Plague Cottages, Eyam

A

1

RILEY
GRAVES

CUCKLET
CHURCH

PLAGUE

COTTAGE

MOMPESSON'S
WELL

HUMPHREY
MERRIL'S
TOMB

C. DANIEL

The Story of Eyam Plague

with a Guide to the Village

Completely Revised 1977
and Enlarged 1983
Revised 1985
Reprinted 1988
Enlarged and Reprinted 1991
Reprinted 1994
© Copyright — all rights reserved.

by

Clarence Daniel

Author of

The Plague Village — Pinnacles of Peak History
A Peakland Portfolio — Derbyshire Ghost Stories, etc.

Published by "Country Bookstore Publications"
Hassop Station, Near Bakewell, Derbyshire DE45 1NW.
Tel. 0629 813444   Fax 0629 814355.   Wholesale distribution same address.

ISBN 0 9523444 0 8

Well Dressing Service, 1965

Courtesy of Glebe Mines Limited.
Photo: "The Derbyshire Times"

CHAPTER ONE

Introducing Eyam

Among the hills, half-buried by the trees,
  And guarded by the craggy knolls which rise
And shelter from the rough untempered breeze,
  Secure and quiet, a little village lies.
Far from the world is this sequestered nook,
  And ancient customs still preserve their sway;
'Twas known to those who wrote in Domesday Book,
  And still the curfew rings at close of day.

(S. L. O'FERRALL)

Situated about 800 ft. above sea-level, the village of Eyam writhes like a serpent of stone cottages at the foot of Sir William Hill (1,419 ft.), sometimes called the 'last mountain in the Pennine Range'. Bit by bit it has been carved from the ridge of sandstone hills above the village, or from the dales which cleave the limestone upon which it stands. It is a village with roots lying deep in the soils of antiquity. Its most venerable monument is the Saxon Cross around which men first gathered to hear the sacred story told by those missionaries who followed wherever the proud Roman eagle had been planted by military conquest. And it is quite probable that men worshipped within its shadow before a church had been raised in Eyam and dedicated to the worship of God. Therefore, the ancient cross is the discarded chrysalis of the Christian faith in Eyam, and remains as a memorial to the forgotten architects who influenced and moulded early religious thought, and laid the foundations upon which the greatness of Britain was built.

Geology The basic rock formations in and around the village are—carboniferous limestone; bituminous, ferruginous and carbonaceous shales; sandstone shales and millstone grit. These rocks largely influence the scenery and determine the vegetation of the district. The limestone is veined with marble, and is rich in metalliferous ores, minerals, corals and fossil formations. Lead, fluorspar, zinc and barytes are among the treasures buried in the hills around Eyam. Traces of copper have also been discovered. Oil, too, exudes from the shales which crop out along the Edge-side escarpment.

In the beginning During the twilight days of prehistory, men established settlements in the neighbourhood of the village, leaving evidence of their occupation in the form of burial mounds, cinerary urns, stone celts, tools and weapons of chipped flint and local chert, and occasional quern-stones and spindle-whorls which recall the domestic habits of these ancient races. Not far away on the moors is the Wet Withins circle which was claimed by popular tradition to have been a centre of Druid ritual and ceremony. It consists of a low circular mound about 100 feet in diameter, with twelve of the original stones still 'in situ', and is said to have formerly contained a large stone in the centre. A little distance away is an impressive cairn of loose stones in which may be seen a cist that was found to contain a large urn enclosing 'burnt bones, ashes, a flint arrow-head, the large beak of a bird and other articles'. On an adjacent moor is a small excavated tumulus in which is embedded a boulder indented with a number of holes. William Wood refers to the former existence of several large stones which composed a circle near Riley, and there are several other smaller examples within the compass of a few miles.

With his weakness for exaggeration, Wood also referred to 'numberless' urns having been found in the vicinity of the village and gives several instances of such discoveries. Several have since been found at Bretton and are now in Weston Park Museum, Sheffield. Another, found in 1912 on the verge of Sir William Road, may be seen in the church vestry and is pathetically in need of restoration.

The discoveries made around Eyam do not suggest density of prehistoric population, or a continuous and settled occupation, and the dispersion of the finds makes it difficult to reconstruct a definite pattern of settlement.

There is also a sparsity of Bronze and Iron Age objects. Ebenezer Rhodes tells of a bronze celt found on Eyam Moor which the local blacksmith foolishly melted down for its metal content! Spindle-whorls and quern-stones have been found, but records of pottery are rare.

Roman coins and sherds of pottery have occasionally been brought to light, while in the Dale a pair of silver armilla (now in Weston Park Museum) were discovered, and in 1814 lime-burners stumbled accidentally upon a hoard of silver and copper coins. The author has found fragments of 'Derbyshire ware' at a site between Eyam and Foolow, together with chipped flints, polishing stones and a lead spindle-whorl. A similar whorl, along with a perforated stone adze, was unearthed by a resident in his garden at New Close Estate, and another had previously been found in a wartime allotment close by, but this was unfortunately lost by the schoolboy finder. A Roman coin and fragments of coarse grey earthenware were dug up when foundations were being prepared for the first houses on this estate. Other coins have been found from time to time, but all these casual discoveries do not add up to actual proof of Roman residence in the village.

But lead (galena) appears to have been the lodestone which drew the first colonists who settled at Eyam, for mining has been so long established in the district that is is uncertain as to whom were the pilgrim fathers of the industry. While civilisation was still young in Britain, the metal was being exported to the imperial city from this part of the remote province of the Roman Empire; and ever since, the fortunes of Eyam have been bound up with this parent industry.

The Romans are known to have worked the 'rakes', or surface veins, as well as extending natural caverns in their search for lead, and coins and fragments of coarse pottery have been found on their spoil heaps. A conical block of this metal, which probably jolted off a wagon or pack-horse carrying smelted 'pigs', or ingots, to some port for shipment to Rome, was found on Eyam Moor many years ago. It weighed 30 lbs. and had a hook or handle attached with which to disengage if from the mould, or to facilitate its easier handling.

The scars of disused mine-hillocks still disfigure the slopes of Eyam Edge which gave its name to the rich vein of ore discovered, or first worked, in the parish at the beginning of the 18th century. Some of these hillocks rather resemble a miniature lunar landscape pitted with craters, mountains and valleys, and are often completely starved of the coarse vegetation which struggles to make some measure of restoration to the disturbed terrain.

Closed in 1884 because of the contemporary recession in lead-mining, the Glebe Mine was re-opened in 1937 in a new prospecting venture for fluorspar, barytes and lead. Demand was increasing for the former mineral in the chemical, glass, enamel, steel and other industries, and for the second in paint, coal, oil drilling and other enterprises. Ladywash Mine was rehabilitated to further explore and exploit the resources of the two mines, while the Sallet Hole drift mine has been recently developed in the Coombs Dale valley. Reserves have been proved by drilling programmes on the Longstone and Hucklow Edges, and old workings are being combed by 'tributers' engaged in opencast recovery of these minerals.

Name   Saxon residents appropriately christened their village as 'a well watered dwelling-place' from the combination of their words *ey*, meaning 'water' and *ham*, the root of that most musical word—'home'! When the Normans surveyed their conquered territory, the scribes entered the name in Domesday Book as Aiune, which may be a misunderstanding of the Saxon way of pronunciation. An inspection of old documents shows how varied has been the spelling through the centuries.

The village has its ancient tenures and its charters, among which is the apocryphal charter granted by King John to miners in the Eyam Mineral Field, sanctioning to them almost unrestricted liberties and privileges in their quest for lead.

The village grew up in a most unselfconscious way, innocent of architectural discipline and unfettered by any restrictions imposed by rural authorities. When necessity arose, or circumstances permitted, the occupants simply added to their cottage a new wing, a bedroom, or an outhouse! Thus the village developed character, distinctiveness and architectural independence. Its rural charm is further enhanced by several dignified houses which disdain to rub shoulders with their humble neighbours, the cottages, but prefer to cultivate the companionship of stately trees where rooks build their nests and where flowers flourish behind high walls. But the homely cottages have no such scruples, and the winding street is fringed with irregular rows and knots of houses built long before the science of house-planning had been evolved. Moreover there has been some domestication of industrial architecture, and several rows of houses—having served the purpose of silk or cotton mills and shoe factories—have later been applied to family needs. These can be recognised by the blocked up widows which provided light for looms and machinery.

But the character of the village is slowly, almost imperceptibly, changing. At one time many of the cottages were thatched, but within the memory of living inhabitants the last three were re-roofed with blue slate. Others are tiled with a local slate which has the subtle quality of harmonizing with the scenic environment, but, unless there is a revival of the now redundant slate-pits near Eyam, we may safely predict that the time will come when the last cottage will be stripped of its stone roof for replacement with one of manufactured tiles or Welsh slate. In the pattern of progress there has also been the inevitable invasion by council estates to replace many an attractive, but perhaps insanitary, cottage swept away by clearance orders. Others have been reprieved and their owners empowered to renovate them to conform with modern standards of comfort and convenience.

Industries   It has been written of Eyam that 'here Antiquity enjoys a deep and mossy sleep', but this atmosphere of somnolence and peace is entirely deceptive, for through the centuries of its existence the village has always been independent and self-supporting. In addition to the lead-mines, employment has been furnished in the past by the dead industries of silk-weaving, cotton spinning and the sandstone quarries; and to-day limestone is still being quarried and such minerals as fluorspar, barytes and lead mined and processed.

Little is recorded or remembered about the cotton industry, nor does it appear to be known when or why the industry was attracted to Eyam. It may have been that the climate was favourable to the industry for it was flourishing before the introduction of mechanisation by hydraulic power. Unlike the neighbouring villages of Calver, Cressbrook and Bamford, where the mills continued on a larger scale until recent times, Eyam had no river to supply its looms with power; although stream water was conserved at Dam Hillock and harnessed for application to the mills in Water Lane. But the village seems to have depended largely on the operation of the hand-loom principle. Such forgotten place-names as Flax Butts are reminiscent of this long dead industry, and one of the trustees of the first Methodist Chapel is described on the deeds as a flax-dresser. R. Murray-Gilchrist, to whom reference will be made later, has an incidental reference to linen manufacture. 'The girl was on the eve of her marriage with a cousin in the Woodlands, and the Pursglove pride dictated that she should take to her new home an ample sufficiency of household linen. In her early days Sarah had spun her own flax and the loom at the Nether End had woven in into sheets and table-cloths of the finest quality; but that was sixty years ago, and now there is neither spinning-wheel nor weaver to be found within twenty miles of the village'.

Richard Furness, the Eyam poet, began his working career as a book-keeper at two small textile factories where "dimity, fustians and cotton goods were

PLAN OF VILLAGE

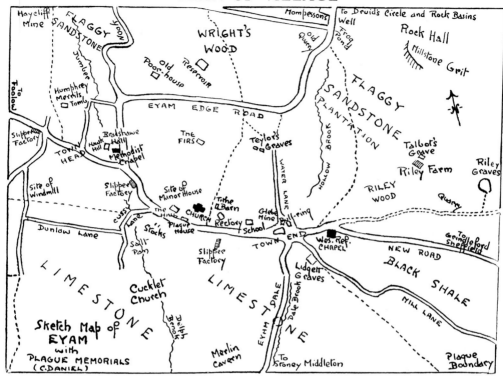

Haycliff Mine · FLAGGY SANDSTONE · Lydon · WRIGHT'S WOOD · Hompessons · To Druid's Circle and Rock Basins · Well · Frog Pond · Rock Hall · Millstone Grit · Old Quarry · Reservoir · Old Poor-house · To Foolow · Humphrey Merrills Tomb · Jumber · Slipper Factory · TOWN HEAD · Eyam Edge Road · The Firs · Teylor's Graves · FLAGGY SANDSTONE PLANTATION · HOLLOW BROOK · Talbot's Grave · Riley Farm · Riley Graves · Bradshawe Hall · Hawk Hill · Methodist Chapel · WATER LANE · RILEY WOOD · Quarry · Site of windmill · Slipper Factory · Site of Manor House · The Hollis · CHURCH · Rectory · Tithe Barn · Glebe Mine · School · Bull-ring · Wes. Ref. Chapel · Grindleford Sheffield · Tolleford · NEW ROAD · Dunlow Lane · Cussy Lane · Stocks · Salt Pan · Plague House · TOWN END · BLACK SHALE · Slipper Factory · EYAM DALE · Lidgett Graves · Dale Brook · MILL LANE · LIMESTONE · Cucklet Church · Delph Brook · LIMESTONE · Merlin Cavern · To Stoney Middleton · Plague Boundary

Sketch Map of
EYAM
with
PLAGUE MEMORIALS
(C. DANIEL)

9

woven', and spent several months mastering the techniques of weaving. William Wood, the village chronicler, was also employed as a hand-loom weaver and studied books secured in a frame attached to his loom. He complained:—'How often while plying my humble and sating trade have I soared on fancy's wings to regions of vision . . . when the entangling of a thread in warp or woof, or the sudden jumping of the shuttle from its stated course, has instantly dissolved the pleasing dream away"

Another William Wood—no relation of the historian—employed in the weaving trade was murdered on July 16th, 1823, when returning home on foot from Manchester where he had sold a quantity of cloth woven in Eyam. He had been paid £60 by bill of exchange and £10 in notes. Viciously attacked by three men whom he had previously treated at an inn, Wood was battered to death on a desolate stretch of moorland road between Disley and Whaley Bridge, and robbed of his money. He was about thirty years of age and left a widow and three children. An inscribed stone by the wayside still identifies the site of the crime.

Even Bradshaw Hall—deserted at the outbreak of the Plague—was pressed into the service of this industry and was seriously damaged by fire while being used as a cotton mill.

Silk was being woven in Eyam at the beginning of last century, but the looms were silent before its close. During the intervening period, however, their clack and clatter made merry music in the village and provided its homes with a measure of modest prosperity. The industry was introduced from Macclesfield and the weavers walked to Tideswell to collect the raw silk from an agent to whom they returned the woven fabrics. Even in those days the village made a small but salutary contribution to the nation's export economy, for exotically coloured scarves were sent to the continent of Africa and eagerly purchased by the coloured tribes. Specimens of silk are still preserved as household treasures in the village and illustrate the variety and imagination of the designs. Gilchrist has a reference to a wedding dress in which the owner says: 'Wain wove th' silk at th' owd factory—et's white wi' a pattron o' forget-me-nots'.

One of the Eyam weavers—Ralph Wain—discovered the art of reproducing patterns on both sides of the material after long and patient experiment and research. Unable to read or write, he forfeited the credit for his invention by selling the idea to a Macclesfield firm. This company offered him a managerial post, but, conscious of his educational defects, Wain declined the offer even though it was renewed with the promise of secretarial help.

Towards the close of last century the shoe manufacturers took over the empty cotton-mills and weaving sheds. The new trade was largely confined to children's footwear, and the early employees operated the apprentice system when orphaned and workhouse children 'lived in'. Shoes were sent abroad at one time and subsidiary factories were established at Hathersage and Bradwell. I make no apology for quoting further from Gilchrist's unofficial and unintentional historical references concerning Eyam, for he was a first-hand observer of some of these now dead industries. He speaks of the women 'binding' the shoe uppers; an employment they were able to follow in spare time in their own homes. 'The women who chatted to each other in the open doorways, knitting socks, or binding children's patent leather slippers for the small shoe factories, shook their heads sympathetically as she went by . . .' Hundreds of children's pump shoes, turn shoes, ankle bands, single and twin bar shoes were produced each day for many years, but wages were low and towards the end of the Great War an agitation for improved pay erupted into a feud between masters and men which developed into a full-scale strike. This spread to the neighbouring village of Stoney Middleton where heavy quarry and farm boots were manufactured. Then, in more recent years, the manufacturers turned their attention in Eyam to adult designs and produced a variety of sophisticated styles for feminine wearers, while one factory concentrated on moulded footwear, but the introduction of plastic shoes caused a gradual recession which resulted in the extinction of the industry.

Limestone quarries have long been worked for road construction material. Old engravings show the fortress-like kilns in the Dale billowing out dense clouds of smoke, but lime-burning is no longer carried out and the kilns are choked with rubbish.

Building stone was provided by several sandstone and gritstone quarries, and ratepayers may still claim the privilege of obtaining their own—free of charge—from several 'town quarries' provided under the terms of the Eyam Enclosure Award of 1817. The local 'slate-pits' produced slabs of laminated sandstone used in roofing and paving houses, but these have long been redundant.

The mushroom growth of Glebe Mines Limited, which became affiliated to Laporte Industries Limited in 1959, is a romance of rural industry. Rehabilitated in 1937 for the mining and treatment of fluorspar, lead and barytes, Glebe Mine was the parent undertaking and was later linked up underground with Ladywash Mine about a mile away. The shaft of this mine was enlarged for the winding of men and material, but the processing plant at Glebe continued to operate until further development was restricted by territorial limits, and the Company found it necessary to transfer its operations to a less restricted site in the adjacent parish of Stoney Middleton, and one more convenient to the sources of opencast material. A new plant—the largest in Europe—was completed in 1935 at a cost of £750,000 and appropriately named Cavendish Mill by the Duke of Devonshire, one of the Lords of the Mineral Field. The offices of the Company were also transferred to the new site, and Eyam Dale House was acquired as its executive headquarters, providing a control centre for the feeding of information whereby management policy is now formulated and the operations of the Company directed.

The uses to which the three minerals are applied are many and varied. Fluorspar, a gangue mineral of galena, is highly valued in the chemical and steel industries. The acid grade is used in the manufacture of hydrofluoric acid, welding rods, aluminium, light alloys, glass and ceramics, while fluorine compounds are used in the production of aerosols, refrigerants, insecticides, etc. Metallurgical grade is used as a fluxing agent for the refinement of steel. Barytes, another gangue mineral of the galena, is processed for use in the manufacture of paints, etc., and is used in colliery washing plants and for oil-drilling operations. Fluorspar is exported to 23 different countries, including Japan and Australia, and the lead is sent to Belgium.

Plague   In his Derbyshire edition of *The King's England* series, Arthur Mee wrote of Eyam: 'It has a fine house, an old church, and in the churchyard one of the finest ancient crosses in the land; it has associations with a group of lettered folk through whom it came to be called the Athens of the Peak. It has its humble cottages, its simple graves, its church not made with hands, its memories of simple folk, and it is with these that its story lives, imperishable'.

The most graphic chapter of village history was unconsciously chronicled by those who carved the few existing stones which overshadow the graves of plague victims. These stones are the fossil remains of a disease buried in the strata of history. But even more than this, they are the punctuation marks in one of the most epic stories in the annals of rural life, and words from the pen of Richard Furness, an Eyam poet, make a fitting epitaph to the memory of those who sleep in the orchards, gardens and meadows of Eyam:-

> Yet still the wild flowers o'er their ashes creep—
> For the cranesbill, pimpernels have grown,
> And the tall ash hangs down in mourning deep,
> Whose roots the rivulet laves, and murmuring seems to weep.

Tercentenary Commemoration   Maximum publicity was given by the national Press, radio and television services to the programme of events which marked the 300th anniversary of the outbreak of plague in the village. At the annual Wells-dressing Festival which inaugurated the proceedings, Lord Hill of Luton performed the opening ceremony and each of the three floral tableaux portrayed some aspect of the plague theme. The adult well was a reproduction of an artist's impression of Mompesson receiving news of the Plague represented in a gilt frame and surrounded by cameos of village scenes and landmarks connected with the Plague story. The general design was conceived by the author who was responsible for draughtmanship of the central panel, while Mrs. Sylvia Dean devised and drew the supporting framework. The children's well was a dramatic copy of an illustration from E. N. Hoare's *The Brave Men of Eyam*, and had been drawn by Mr. D. Kyme, while at the Town Head well Miss Mary Colley had chosen the subject of Job's affliction and deliverance from disease.

The 'Plague Sunday' service in Cucklet Delph attracted a record attendance and the preacher was the Rt. Rev. Dr. D. Coggan, then Archbishop of York. A fortnight's performance of Monica Thorne's play, *The Sweet Air*, was staged in a marquee in the grounds of Eyam Dale House and was presented to capacity audiences. The cast was largely drawn from the village and the producer was Dr. L. du Garde Peach who lived in the civil and ecclesiastical parish of Eyam.

The final performance was staged for the benefit of Glebe Mines Limited on the evening of the official opening of Cavendish Mill, and the audience included Lord and Lady Hill of Luton, the Duke of Devonshire and Count and Countess Guilini, of Milan, in addition to other distinguished guests and overseas visitors.

Plague Literature   Eyam's epic story of the Plague has made the village a national shrine of pilgrimage. Ever increasing numbers have become acquainted with this tragic, but triumphant, story of a shrinking community of ordinary people who became extra-ordinary in accepting voluntary isolation and facing the prospect of virtual annihilation that they might preserve the inhabitants of neighbouring townships from exposure to the horrors they endured. Such a shining story of courage and self-sacrifice has naturally excited the admiration, stimulated the imagination, and inspired the pen of poets, dramatists, novelists and journalists whose praises have created a considerable accumulation of literature over the years. Many of the vast number of articles subscribed to periodicals, magazines and journals have, on the other hand, had little chance of survival owing to the ephemeral existence of such literature.

The village will always be indebted to William Wood, the self-taught chronicler who studied the arts of writing and rhetoric to publicise the proud story of his native village, and the several editions of his *History and Antiquities of Eyam* have provided the basic information concerning the Plague. Ebenezer Rhodes, in his *Peak Scenery*, supplied another useful source of information from which Wood himself drew material.

William and Mary Howitt, Dr. J. C. Holland, Samuel Roberts, Richard Furness, 'an Old Blue' and Mrs. S. L. O'Ferrall were among those who helped to immortalise the story in poetry and prose. Playwrights who have applied the story to dramatic art include Monica Thorne (*The Sweet Air*), Joyce Denning (*Isolation at Eyam*) and Alex Wilson (*The Wick and the Wax*). In the earlier days of sound broadcasting, when emotional appeal had to be induced by vocal and not visual effects, the B.B.C. dramatised the story in a moving play entitled 'The Epic of Eyam', and has also brought the story to the attention of listening audiences during its educational programmes for schools. With such ready-made ingredients of romance and tragedy, simple faith and reluctant heroism, more dramatists have recognised the potential of the story. Alan Cullen, a member of the Sheffield Playhouse Company, achieved considerable success with his 'Ring o' Roses' which had its world premiere in 1967 in the nearby city of Sheffield. Don Taylor's 'The Roses of Eyam' had its world premiere in 1970 at the Northcott Theatre, Exeter, and later still John Haggerty's 'A Plague on all the houses' was staged at Derby. 'The Roses of Eyam' has currently been adapted for television.

Each play and each novel has added to the Plague story some inspired accretion of artistic imagination, or seized upon a name from the list of victims to endow a character with self-conceived vices or virtues, whereupon the impressionable play-goer or reader often accepts them as genuine Plague personalities.

13

Fact and fancy are interwoven in the works of fiction written by such novelists as E. N. Hoare (*The Brave Men of Eyam*), Joseph Hatton (*The Dagger and the Cross*), Marjorie Bowen (*God and the Wedding Dress*), Roy Meldrum (*The Wooing of Margaret Trevenna*) and Helen Shipton (*The Herons*).

Illustrations Several illustrations in this booklet are of a rather novel character, in that they are photographs of some of the floral pictures created during our annual wells-dressing festivals. For several years the floral tableaux have represented some particular phase of village history, and were designed by the author to combine thanksgiving for water with an appreciation of personalities who, by the nobility of their lives, the exercise of outstanding gifts, or the courage with which they faced danger and death; have made the village a shrine of pilgrimage to lovers of history and the arts of poetry, painting, music and literature.

The first venture in this direction was the portrayal of the Saxon Cross in 1954. Encouraged by the success of this effort, the village church was depicted in this novel medium and succeeding pictures have portrayed such village landmarks as Mompesson's Well, the birth-place of Richard Furness, Plague Cottages, the village Hall and Rectory, and the Windmill which was demolished in 1877. In 1956 a specially designed well was prepared for a visit of the British Association and this showed the chancel door and sundial of the church. They have been pages in an album of flowers which, year by year, told something of the Story of Eyam.

Visit of H.R.H. Prince of Wales

CHAPTER TWO

Guide to the Village

Introduction. The Church. Leaving the Church and churchyard, we call at the Rectory and next visit Bagshaw House—Plague Cottage—Delf View—Brick House—the Stocks—Eyam Hall—Cucklet Church—Home of Margaret Black-well—Bradshaw Hall—Orchard Bank—a Poet's birthplace—Hollin's House and its lonely tomb.

Introduction Almost every house in Eyam has a history, and each mansion some memory of romance or mystery, and this *Guide* has been designed with the object that its reader may see as much of the village as possible in the least time. It also aims at giving the maximum amount of information concerning the various places of interest; so, for the convenience of those who have little time to spend in the village, the actual route has been printed in italics, the places visited in bold type, and the historical notes in ordinary print.

By adopting this method it is hoped that if you have little time to study the *Guide* on the spot, you may find your visit made more profitable by reading the historical comments on some subsequent occasion. And more than this, at some time in the future—perhaps in winter when the landscape is drained of colour and the hedges and trees are etched against a background of snow; when the robin haunts your threshold and logs blaze on the hearth—the perusal of this *Guide* will recall your visit to Eyam, and you may visualise its gray Church, its sturdy cottages, and its graves among the celandines and daisies.

A word of warning may be interposed here concerning the tablets attached to some houses and purporting to supply information on the occupants at the time of the Plague. Apart from the well authenticated sites, the claims of these should not be taken too literally. They were introduced during the Festival of Britain as an added interest and attraction, but cannot be verified by actual documentary or other evidence.

The Church is an interesting and imposing edifice to the student of architecture, but its charm for the average visitor lies not so much in the dignity of its structural proportions—mellowed as they are with age—but in the historical associations which made the village famous. Apart from the south wall of the chancel, the stone used in its construction is a tawny sandstone quarried from the hills behind the village. Much of the masonry is discoloured and mottled with tints of green moss, while some of the softer stones are peeling

15

as the result of erosion. The south wall of the chancel is built of grey limestone stained with age and chequered with an occasional square of sandstone. In places it is piped with white mortar where the stones have been freshly pointed. This wall was formerly covered with ivy, but now only a few rambler roses cling at intervals to the wall, and a clematis overhangs the doorway, adding a pleasing touch of colour to this ancient portion of the fabric.

The embattled tower is surmounted by four crocketted pinnacles, two of which were removed in 1944 because of their state of decay. For some years the tower remained with only the two northern pinnacles, but the balance was restored by the erection of replicas on the south side. The older pinnacles are of equal age to the grotesque gargoyles which adorn each angle of the tower, peering down as though keeping vigil over every approach to the church. They remind us of the days when religion had not been completely divorced from superstition, because, instead of being a true reflection of the sculptor's skill, they were deliberately made ugly in order to frighten away evil spirits. These amulets of stone do, however, serve a more practical purpose in that they also drain away rain water from the tower roof.

During its long history, the church has been much altered and restored. The tower was enlarged in 1618 when the pinnacles, gargoyles, battlements and beading of the earlier tower were incorporated in the present structure. Four of the six bells were cast at the beginning of the 17th century, and the other two were added in 1926. A major restoration was carried out in 1868-9 at a cost of £2,160, and a further one in 1883 costing £660.

Saxon Church? It is thought that a church has existed on this foundation since Saxon times, and a claim has been made that the two pillars between the nave and north aisle are of Norman origin and rest on Saxon bases. In the north aisle is a **Saxon Font,** but this is a comparatively recent acquisition from Brookfield Manor, Hathersage, where it did service in the garden as a flower bowl.

Norman Church? Domesday Book makes no reference to either a church or priest at Eyam, and Dr. Cox reached the conclusion that "there is nothing of the Norman period about the building, unless it be the ancient font . . . which is of a plain circular design'. The **Norman Font** was shorn of its antiquary interest and value by an unimaginative mason who planed away the carving from its bowl when instructed to clean it of paint. It will also be noted that there is no drain; a fact which recalls those days when the water was only blessed twice a year and was kept under lock and key regardless of its possible contamination.

It has been suggested that a Norman church, occupying the site of the original Saxon building, existed for two centuries before the erection, in the Decorated style, of the present fabric which has since undergone much remodelling, extension and enlargement. Fragmentary portions of this 14th century church have survived the subsequent restorations. Both the pillars, arches and masonry of the nave are very old, in spite of careful renovation which gives the impression that they are comparatively new. The capitals of the pillars; pointed arches on each side of the nave; the archway into the tower, and windows of the bell-chamber in the tower, are all of the Decorated period. A small doorway in the west wall of the tower also belonged to this period, but has since been built up and substituted by a two-light window. The south side of the chancel is lighted by three lancet windows of the Early English period. Two others may be seen at the west end of the north aisle, but only one is original; the other being inserted at the 1868-69 restoration. The two-light windows of the north aisle—inserted in 1868-69—are also of Decorated design, and were copied from the original window in this aisle.

The clerestory windows on the north side of the nave are genuine Perpendicular; those on the opposite side being enlarged and made to correspond with them at the final restoration in 1882, before which they were glazed with square panes. The semi-circular relieving arches beneath them were exposed in 1962. Of the original 18 tie-beams which supported the roof, three have been preserved, and the carved end-bosses of the others were formerly retained in the recesses of the chancel roof, but had to be removed because of the danger of wood infection.

Murals During the year 1962, masons carrying out an examination of defective plaster in the nave exposed traces of three superimposed schemes of mural painting. The earliest period was dated as belonging to the second half of the 16th century and consisted of a series of twelve cartouches representing the emblems, or symbols, of the Twelve Tribes of Israel, with appropriate quotations from Jacob's blessing painted in heavy Gothic lettering. The series was indentified by Mr. E. Clive Rouse who compared the work to that of Burton Latimer and West Walton.

Above this early series, traces of a re-painting of the same scheme were detected at a different level and of a later period concluded to be Jacobean, while they had been covered by a scheme incorporating the Creed and Lord's Prayer framed in elaborate scroll-work. This rediscovery of the murals recalled the Plague Bicentenary restoration when they were previously uncovered. Dr. J. C. Cox wrote that 'a good many wall-frescoes were brought to light during the alterations, but they were not of a nature to withstand exposure'. This assumption has been disproved by the excellent and expert restoration of the Naphtali cartouche on the north wall carried out by Mrs. Eve Baker.

Three galleries were removed from the church in 1868-69.

Objects of Interest The Church has its museum interest.

The Jacobean **Pulpit** has fortunately survived the various restorations, although it was moved in 1868 from the opposite side of the nave to its present position, and the old clerk's seat abolished. It was occupied by both Stanley and Mompesson.

In the chancel may be seem **Mompesson's Chair.** Made of oak, the chair is carved with the inscription *Mom 1662 Eyam*. It was rescued from a Liverpool antique shop by the Rev. Canon E. Hacking, a former rector, and presented to the church. The panel in the back is carved with a crude representation of the Virgin and Child. In the west end of the north aisle may be seen the alleged **Plague Chest** which is supposed to have contained the infected materials sent from London, and which appears to have been subsequently used as a cupboard in the Plague Cottage. The history of this relic seems altogether vague and unsupported by definite proof. Under a glass case in the rector's vestry can be seen a Bronze Age **Cinerary Urn** which was found on Sir William Hill. Its discovery is described in the 1912 edition of the *Derbyshire Archaeological Journal*.

Also in the rector's vestry hangs a bronze lamp of Tudor origin, which, if genuinely connected with the church should repose in the north aisle, for it was presented with the claim that it is the original Lamp of St. Helen kept burning on the altar as a condition of tenure whereby the Staffords held certain properties in the district. Legend tells of the lamp being kept fuelled by the apocryphal Margaret Stafford when she was temporarily exiled from her home.

Dr. Cox queried the statement by Ebenezer Rhodes that "the estate was conferred on the family by the crown in recognition of certain military services, and that it was held on 'condition that a lamp should be kept perpetually burning before the altar of St. Helen in the parish church of Eyam'," and wrote: 'We have taken considerable trouble to try and test the truth of this statement, and all that we can say is that we have hitherto met with no corroboration'.

We find unimpeachable truth of the existence of the lamp, however, in the manuscript department of the British Museum where two 13th century documents provide evidence of three bovates of land in Eyam granted by Eustace de Morteyne to Richard Stafford and his heirs to be held 'by hereditary right, free, undisturbed, and intact wholly and severally in their locality and pertaining to the aforesaid village within and without for the sole purpose of providing one lamp burning before the altar of St. Helen, in the Church of Eyam, throughout the year while Divine Service is conducted in the said church. This duty frees them from all other duties to me and my heirs'. The second deed concerns the conveyance of the above property to Roger, son of the aforesaid Richard, on the condition stipulated by the father that 'as long as I live I be allowed to exact and demand afterwards the means for performing the duty I have been wont to perform, to wit, to provide one lamp burning before the altar of St. Helen the Virgin, in the Church of Eyam, throughout the year while Divine Service is conducted in the said Church'.

The Chapel of St. Helen is said to have been founded by one of the Staffords and endowed with a gift of wax to be used in keeping alight the lamp. The chapel consisted of the north aisle which was largely occupied by the Stafford-Bradshaw pew, and when this was dismantled a century ago some of the woodwork was used for the construction of the present belfry and chancel screens.

Other alterations to the church included an extension of the chancel, and this made the **Squint** inaccurate. This aperture pierces the masonry of the N.E. wall of the south aisle immediately behind the pulpit and was cut through in 1908 at the expense of the Burdekins whose family pew was in the south aisle, and who, because of the pulpit and projecting masonry, were unable to visually participate in parts of the service conducted in the chancel. This expedient gave rise to the popular legend of the 'leper's squint'. Another squint, which slanted through the angle of the wall between the north aisle and chancel, was blocked up by the restorers in 1868 and may have served as a confessional in pre-Reformation times.

In the choir vestry, among the collection of portraits of past rectors, is a reproduction of an oil painting of the Rev. William Mompesson, the original of which is at Southwell Minster. A gold framed miniature is also in the custody of a former Rector. At the east end of the south aisle will be seen a glass case mounted on a stand. This contains a document inscribed with a list of plague victims, and has been produced in illuminated style with cameos of the Church and Plague Cottages.

Leaving the Church we find **Mrs. Mompesson's Tomb** just beyond the Saxon Cross. Bearing a Latin inscription, the tombstone is of crumbling sandstone and is guarded at each corner with a champhered pillar. On the top of the table may be seen a small square of stone sunk into the surface. It denotes a mistake made in the inscription which necessitated a neat 'correction' being made by the mason.

Only one other plague gravestone has survived in the churchyard and is reared against the east wall of the south aisle. It is to the memory of one of the early victims, Abell Rowland, who died on the 15th January, 1666.

It is scarcely necessary to draw attention to the **Saxon Cross**—the most venerable landmark in the village. For over a thousand years it has stood shelterless and bareheaded, exposed to the ravages of wind and rain, the wayside witness to an imperishably story. Perhaps this simple translation of the Gospel was being wrought out of living stone about the same time that a spark of inspiration kindled the emotions of Caedmon at Whitby. Fortunately it escaped mutilation when Puritan zealots were authorised by an act of Parliament passed in 1643 to remove and destroy 'all crosses in any open place', although the top portion of the shaft has since been broken up and used for cobble stone. Until the visit of John Howard, the prison reformer, it lay almost smothered by weeds in a corner of the churchyard, but his concern for the preservation of such a valuable relic inspired its erection in a more prominent position.

Mercia was evangelized by missionaries from Lindisfarne, or Holy Island, and the Eyam cross resembles in certain characteristics the type for which Iona is famous. Upon the head and arms, figures of angels are sculptured in relief; whilst the upper portion of the shaft is adorned with a representation of the Virgin and Child, beneath which is a figure holding a trumpet, or bugle-horn. Below these pictorial panels is an elaborate tracery of scroll-work woven into three circles. The carving on the reverse of the shaft consists of five foliated scrolls in each of which a trefoil design is cleverly triplicated.

19

Rev. Thomas Seward
Courtesy of Mr. K. Gregory

Miss Anna Seward
Courtesy of Mr. K. Gregory

William Wood (Eyam Historian)

Few monuments have been reproduced in a greater variety of artistic media. It was depicted in lichens, mosses and cones at the 1954 wells-dressing festival, and copied in plaster-covered cardboard for a carnival tableau illustrating the introduction of the Christian faith to Eyam. It can be seen embroidered on the G.F.S. banner in Church, and was embossed in gilt on the covers of certain editions of William Wood's *History of Eyam*, and also on those of Sir Francis Chantrey's selection of *Peak Scenery* engravings. Porcelain models of the cross—the larger type being surprisingly true to detail—could once be purchased in Eyam. Indeed, it has become so symbolical of the village that it was chosen for the design of the special franking device used to cancel stamps during the Plague Tercentenary commemoration. And it has been sketched, painted and photographed on innumerable occasions.

Above the chancel door may be seen the **Sun-dial** which has recently been cleaned. Previous to the erection of the porch, this elaborate piece of crafts-manship in stone was mounted over the doorway to the south aisle and was protected by a pediment. Its complex features have been described as follows:- 'A vertical plane declining westward, and from certain mathematical principles connected with conic sections, the parallels of the sun's meridian altitude—an azimuthal scale—the points of the compass, and a number of meridians are well delineated on the plane from the stereographic projection of the sphere. The plane being large, the horary scale is well divided; the upper or fiducial edge of the style is brass, and an indentation therein, representing the centre of the projection, casts the light or shade of its point on the hyperbolic curves and other furniture of the dial'. It also gives the relative times at London, Jerusalem, Mecca, Mexico and other parts of the world when it is noon at Eyam. The design was by a Mr. Duffin, clerk to Mr. Simpson, of Stoke Hall, and it was executed by a local stone-mason named William Shore. It also bears the names of the contemporary churchwardens. Above the dial is inscribed the Latin maxim: *Induce animum sapientum* (To excite a wise or enquiring mind), and it is supported by two projecting corbels which state: *Ut umbra sic vita* (As a shadow, so is life).

Just over the east wall of the churchyard is the **Rectory.** In 1960 a major re-modelling of the Rectory was carried out so that the house would conform with modern standards of comfort and convenience. This operation involved the demolition of the ponderous three-storied Georgian wing built in the prosperous times of the Rev. Thomas Seward, Rector of Eyam and Canon of Lichfield Cathedral, together with some derelict kitchen premises which had long been sealed off from the rest of the building. The earlier portion of the house, which had been occupied by the Plague heroes, Stanley and Mompesson, was retained and incorporated in the re-designed building. During the process of alteration, the ancient glass of the diamond-paned study window, and part of that in the staircase window, suffered irreparable damage by workmen neglecting to take elementary precautions against its breakage, and most of the panes had to be substituted with 'reproduction' glass.

The building had assumed its exaggerated proportions to accommodate the family and large domestic staff of the Rev. Thomas Seward who enjoyed the living during the days of lead-mining affluence. With the discovery in 1717 of the rich Edgeside Vein, the value of the living rocketed from a modest £150 to £1,600 per year, and, at the peak of mining prosperity, the figure reached £1,800 as a result of revenue from tithes. Such an attractive stipend created some competition for the pulpit of Eyam Church, and the contemporary list of rectors includes several titled names.

The Hon. Dr. Edward Finch, fifth son of Sir Heneage Finch, Keeper of the Great Seal, and afterwards Baron Finch of Daventry, and Earl of Nottingham, surrendered the living of Wigan to minister in Eyam from 1717 to 1738. His memory is perpetuated by the communion plate which he gave to the church, and by a charity disbursed each year to thirteen widows and spinsters. The Hon. Thomas Bruce, second son of the Earl of Kincardine, held the living for only one year and died in France in 1739.

Next followed the Rev. Thomas Seward who built the imposing Georgian wing. His daughter, Anna, who became renowned as the 'Swan of Lichfield', was born in the Rectory and spent her childhood days in Eyam. Seward was also a canon of Lichfield Cathedral and, favouring the more genteel society of that city, largely left the care of Eyam parish to his curate, the poetical Rev. Peter Cunningham. Amongst the friends of the Sewards were Dr. Johnson, the lexicographer, who described the Rector as a "valetudinarian'; John Howard, the prison reformer, Dr. Erasmus Darwin, the poet and naturalist, and other prominent persons. Miss Seward's poetry proved a phenomenal success and rival publishers competed for the privilege of presenting to the public edition after edition of her poetical and epistolatory works. Yet these scarcely survived her own generation and are now relegated to the obscurity of reference library shelves. In her will she appointed a reluctant Sir Walter Scott as editor of her posthumous works. She was painted by George Romney and by Tilly Kettle in 1762, both paintings having been engraved as frontispiece illustrations for her works. The later portrait can be seen in the National Portrait Gallery. Her father's portrait was painted by Joseph Wright, of Derby, and that of her mother by Sir Peter Lely.

The painting by Romney was delivered at Lichfield on May 31st, 1788, and the next day Miss Seward sent a grateful letter to the poet, William Haley, for using his good offices in securing the services of the artist to carry out the commission for the benefit of her aged father. This painting is now in America, but a reproduction is preserved in the files of the National Portrait Gallery. A bust engraving of this portrait was used as frontispiece illustration to 'The Beauties of Miss Seward'. What must be a copy of this portrait—for the pose is identical—was used as frontispiece illustration to Hesketh Pearson's 'The Swan of Lichfield (Anna Seward)', and is qualified by the sub-title 'After the Portrait by Romney'. Comparison of the two portraits shows distinct differences in the features of the subject, her head-dress, hair style and dress accessories, as well as in the draperies and background. Whereas the original has a book, quill and ornamental vase on the table, and a classical landscape, the copy shows a quill, ink-well and documents.

The value of the living was shrinking during this period, and Miss **Seward** wrote in 1786 that 'the value of Eyam living to my father, once near £700 per annum, is not now more than £150'.

Although the Rev. Charles Hargreaves did not make any great impact upon contemporary society, he was involved in a history-making business speculation while at Eyam. He and several influential neighbours provided the capital for the first steamship service to operate on the River Mersey at Liverpool, and the first vessel to carry passengers was named *The Elizabeth* in honour of his daughter. The venture did not prove financially successful, but it had a romantic sequel when Elizabeth married her cousin, Colin Watson, who had largely conceived and pioneered the project.

Following the Hargreaves in 1822, the Hon. Robert Eden—said to be an ancestor of Sir Anthony Eden—was Rector for four years. He was later Chaplain to King William IV and to Queen Victoria, and became Bishop of Sodor and Man in 1847, and Bishop of Bath and Wells in 1854. He succeeded to the title of 3rd Lord Auckland.

It was probably the children of the Rev. E. B. Bagshaw who had the little pointed stone carved with the inscription *Hic cumbit Psittacus qui oo mane Martii quini ano dni* 1847 to identify the grave of their pet parrot. And the stone can still be seen in the masonry of the east wall of the re-designed Rectory.

A little lower down the village and opposite the school is Eyam Dale House, the house illustrated in colour on the frontispiece page. This is now the headquarters of the Glebe Mines company of the Laporte Industries group. It has been enlarged from time to time, but always with careful attention to the choice of matching material and with the object of preserving architectural harmony. It was the home of Thomas Birds, an antiquary whose collection was partly acquired by Weston Park Museum, Sheffield. Many well-known personalities in business, professional, political and sporting spheres (including royal guests), have been entertained in this village 'stately home'.

Returning to the churchyard we now leave by the path skirting the War Memorial, and notice a cottage across the road with a large bay window. This is the reputed home of the Wragg family, members of which were among the early victims of the Plague. For many years it served as Post Office, but has now been restored with great care and consideration for its environment. A grave-stone found beneath these premises was mentioned by William Wood and is to the memory of Alice Wragg, but it was probably a stone-mason's 'reject' in that the inscription has two dating errors.

Next door is another trim cottage with white-painted door and shining brass knocker. Its tiny garden is surrounded by a low brick wall from which bristle a row of spear-like railings. Now known as **Bagshawe House,** it is the reputed cottage where death thwarted the bridal preparations of Emmot Siddal at the time of the Plague. It was formerly thatched and its original architecture has been much changed by structural improvements.

Almost opposite Bagshaw House we see three picturesque cottages renowned for their associations with the Plague. The middle one—its few square yards of garden refreshed each spring with snowdrops and crocuses—seems to shrink from publicity, yet ever since the dark days of 1665-66 it has been distinguished as the **Plague Cottage**—the home of the first victim. Artists have sketched and painted it, and we find it prominent in many a photographer's album. It, too, has been extensively rebuilt and only the kitchen retains its identity with the seventeenth century.

An amusing anecdote is recalled concerning a former tenant—an eccentric fellow who had his coffin made during his lifetime. This he kept stored underneath his bed, and occasionally would indulge his fancy by draping himself in a shroud and spending the night in the coffin! The accounts of the village undertaker contained an entry respecting repairs done to the coffin and for the supply of a new shroud.

William Wood tells another humorous story concerning a former occupant who was a veteran soldier living in retirement at the cottage. His name was Adam Holmes and he had distinguished himself in the Napoleonic wars, losing his left leg at Waterloo, and having his military career brought to a proud close when a firing party visited the village to discharge a farewell volley at his graveside.

Holmes had one day been examining a defective flue in the kitchen and found a pair of ancient leather stays concealed in a crevice in the chimney. His heart quailed as he gingerly withdrew the article of female figure control from its place of hiding, fearing that it might have been hidden there at the close of the Plague by some fair owner reluctant to part with such a proud possession. Holmes committed the stays to the garden for burial with all speed!

A few paces beyond, on the opposite side of the road, we notice the blank wall of what is actually one of the most pleasantly situated houses in Eyam—the **Delf View**. Its lawns are velvety; its trees among the most aristocratic in the village, and it commands an unrivalled view of the Cucklet Delph. For many years this charming Georgian residence was the home of Frederick Dawson, a pianist of international reputation whose genius exalted him to a position of rivalry with Paderewski. Although the admirers of Mr. Dawson were of mixed speech and nationality, they all recognised his eloquence in the world-wide language of music. He was particularly popular in Germany. His wife painted pictures and wrote several novels including 'The Virgin and the Scales' and 'The Upper Hand'. The house had other literary associations and was occupied by the owners of a Sheffield newspaper at one period.

It is reliably claimed that Joseph Wright, of Derby, who was an artist celebrated for his studies by moonlight and artificial light, painted his portrait of Sarah Carver and her young daughter at Delf View. She was wife of the Rev. J. Carver who held the living of Eyam towards the close of the 17th and the beginning of the eighteenth century, and was daughter of Thomas and Elizabeth Allen of Eyam. Her mother was a member of the Middleton family of Leam Hall, and the portrait was presented to Derby Art Gallery by the late Mrs. G. Rose Innes, of Leam Hall, who was descended from the same family.

Passing a little further along the street our attention is drawn to a large, square house built of brick and roofed with local stone. This is the **Brick House,** so distinguished because it used to be the only house in Eyam built of this material. The bricks, which have been sobered in colour by passing years and which do not afflict the eye with a sense of injury or outrage, are said to have been made locally. For many years a metal plaque, adorned with a benevolent looking sun—the symbol of a well-known insurance company—was fixed above the door, reminding us of the days when insurance companies provided their own fire engines and equipment. If, upon being summoned to a fire, the crew of one of these private engines found that the building was insured by a rival company, it was not improbable that they would whip up their horses and drive away!

Nearby are the village **Stocks** which were restored in 1951 to mark the Festival of Britain. This part of the village is known as The Cross and the shuttered building is the **Market House** where farmers sold their butter, eggs and poultry. It is not unlikely that the miners also bargained with metal merchants for their lead. A market Cross may have stood here, or even the Saxon Cross. Tradition claims that the latter stood on the verge of the old Sheffield-Manchester road crossing Sir William Hill, and another possible site is that of Crosslow, the highest point overlooking the village from the west.

Those who seek harmony in architecture will not be disappointed in **Eyam Hall** across the way. This mansion is approached by three semi-circular steps leading through an elegant ball-topped gateway—dignified with wrought iron gates which replaced the rather clumsy wooden ones some years ago—and across a broad pavement to the flight of worn stone steps where tufts of fern grow in the crevices. Time has mellowed and tinted the ancient stones of the Hall, and cream coloured roses peep through mullioned windows into the spacious rooms within. Its leaded lights are filled with diamonds and squares of greenish glass which soberly reflect the changing colours of the sky. Romance is written in the form of a poem on one of these panes, while on another someone has inscribed with a diamond the crest and arms of the Wright family.

Some writers claim that in the year 1676, while the Plague was still a vivid memory in Eyam, the Hall was partially rebuilt. This date is embossed on the leaden fall-pipes. William Wood says: 'A new front was erected and other alterations made about 1680. In the interior, on some wainscoting there are inscribed the initials F.B. and J.B., with the date 1594 or 6. The exterior contains an inverted stone with the initials M.B., beside other mementoes of the Brays of Eyam'. The inscription appears to be the same to which Dr. Cox refers when quoting a Sheffield antiquary concerning the Stafford-Bradshaw pew: 'On the pew, where this quire or enclosure formerly stood, there was the inscription 'J.B. 1595 F.B.'; the letters being the initials of John Bradshaw and Francis Bradshaw'.

Wood's contention that the house was formerly occupied by the Brays and purchased from this family by the Wrights about the middle of the seventeenth century, is disputed by the present owner, Mr. C. S. Wright, who has evidence that it was built in 1676 by his ancestor, Thomas Wright. Although Tudor in style, it was built in Stuart times.

An excellent description of the Hall is contained in Roy Meldrum's novel, 'The Wooing of Margaret Trevenna', and reads:- 'And between the three, they made an idyllic estate, small as it was, of that Hall among the hills, that house over the broad grey wall in the village street, with its long low front, its two wings slightly projecting, its long sturdy windows passing the light into the low rooms, the wide flight of steps to the door, the square dignified chimneys, the amber roof tiles, the quaint spouts, the depth of its flank, three gables deep, the roses and creepers, scarlet in autumn, and golden lichen, which gave colour to its green grey stones, the circular steps down to the high-walled garden, the lawn and the wealth of flowers according to season, lavender, rosemary, stocks, roses, the flower of rivalry between the Rector and the Squire, columbine, mignonette, marigold, nasturtium, marguerites; yew trees, which stood before the house was built beyond them under the Tudors, and the fruit trees of the kitchen garden'.

Across the road from the Hall is a house which figured in one of Robert Murray Gilchrist's short stories, 'Lucretia at the Cabal House'. It can still be recognised in the following description:- 'It stands on the west side of Milton Green, facing the stocks—a white-washed cottage with sharpe gables, which had been built long before the Plague travelled from London to harass Milton. It was Dan's own property, inherited from his father. The small silk factory outside the village, which his mother had brought into the Twigg family had been let to a shoe warehouseman . . . ' The small silk factory, since enlarged, may be seen at the top of the village and has since done service as a shoe factory.

Readers intending to visit **The Delph** *must obtain the key from the Hall and are politely requested to apply at the kitchen door which is reached through the wooden gates. Proceeds of the small charge for admission are devoted to charity. Unlocking the gate in the railings behind the stocks, we enter a strip of land once known as the* **Toothill** *and which is claimed to be the site of an altar or shrine consecrated by the Druids to the worship of Teutates, or Tuisti, the Celtic god of war whose name survives in our Tuesday. Hathersage and many other villages and town ships have their toothills said to be connected with the worship of this ancient deity. We soon reach a steep declivity leading into the Delph—a valley dedicated to peace and tranquillity, and undefiled by the quarryman's quest for stone. In the words of Arthur Mee, it is 'a haunt of peace and loveliness among the trees which June had filled with the song of birds and the joy of flowers'. Descending the steep slopes of the valley to the rivulet which emerges from a narrow limestone gorge called the Salt Pan, we climb the opposite side and bear left over the shoulder of a grassy knoll to the cavern known as* **Cucklet Church.**

It was here that the dwindling number of parishioners gathered for worship after the village church had been closed to prevent the spread of infection. and here in the stillness, unbroken, except for the twitter of birds or the rattle of a pebble dislodged by our uncertain feet, we stand in awe to think that the voice of Mompesson reverberated through the arches of this weird church and crept in dying echoes into the now deserted cloisters. What memories must lie buried in this cold stone tomb!

Retracing our steps to the Hall where we return the key, we next continue along the street until it curves to the left. Facing down the street is the door of a cottage which is the reputed home of **Margaret Blackwell**—a girl who recovered from the plague after drinking hot bacon fat while in a state of feverish delirium.

A short distance beyond we may catch a glimpse of the ruined fragment of **Bradshaw Hall** immediately behind the Methodist Chapel. Widowed of its former pride and stateliness, this fragment of Tudor architecture retained some snatches of its dignity until a few years ago when it collapsed into a heap of rubble. Somewhere among the debris which cascaded to the ground is a carved stone bearing the crest of the Bradshaw family. Built of sandstone mellowed by the centuries, and with tufts of yellow stonecrop clinging to its decaying masonry and splashing its moss-tinted roof with patches of gold, its crumbling architecture stood like the mausoleum of some forgotten family in a neglected graveyard of the past.

Inside, the building was but an empty shell. Floors had been torn out and windows blocked with masonry. Generations of swallows had built their nests under the naked slates and rats scampered across gaping floor-boards beneath which cows jostled each other in the gloomy basement. Great fires had once blazed upon the hearths, filling the rooms with warmth and comfort, but the carved stone fire-places had long been empty and cold. Even the ghosts of the old families seemed to have forsaken the derelict mansion.

Bradshaw Hall was erected as an extension of Stafford Hall by Francis Bradshaw, great grandson of that Francis who in 1565 had married Anne, one of the four daughters of Humphrey Stafford—the last of the male line of his family. Few particulars have been preserved concerning the former mansion except that it was built during the reign of Henry VI; had a flat roof covered with lead; floors of polished black oak; and a large room, the beams of which were ornamented with heraldic carvings, and which was lighted by a traceried window facing east. Above the door a circular stone bore the Stafford crest—*a chevron between three martlets.* When this mansion was demolished, the new wing appears to have been left intact and became known as the hall of the Bradshaws. It was deserted, evidently before completion, by the widow and daughter of Squire George Bradshaw who fled from the plague, and tradition says that the tapestries which were intended to adorn the walls mouldered away without ever being hung. It was later occupied by several families, and William Wood tells of a stone in the churchyard bearing the inscription:-

'Here lieth the Body of John, the son of John and Mary Morton, of Bradshaw Hall, who departed this life June 18, 1762'.

Eventually the hall was deserted and did service as a cotton mill for some time, being severely damaged by fire while fulfilling this purpose. It was then abandoned to the farmer, his cattle, and his crops. The stone medallion embossed with the Bradshaw crest—*a stag at gaze p.p.r. standing under a vine fructed p.p.r.*—occupied a position between the second storey windows facing south. Nearby is the **Hawk Hill** where the family indulged in the sport of falconry. It is a flat, semi-circular elevation with steeply dipping sides.

Typical Plague
Commemoration Service.

Scene from "The Sweet Air"
1965.

Courtesy of Glebe Mines Limited.
Photo: "The Derbyshire Times"

A now vanished landmark—the Windmill—occupied a prominent position across from the old Hall. It was pulled down before 1877 and the masonry of the tower was used in building the present school. Before its final demolition and while in a semi-ruinous state, Eyam's self-taught artist—John Platts— painted the mill from several angles to preserve a faithful 'likeness' of the once proud landmark. By the number of such surviving paintings, Platts must have received numerous commissions to reproduce the picture. He was also sufficiently far-sighted to recognise that the removal of this building would rob the Peak District of what was possibly its only remaining example of this type of industrial architecture, and urgently petitioned in poetry for its reprieve from the sentence of demolition. But, alas, in vain, and now only the adjacent corn store and an odd grinding-stone remains near a circular garden which identifies the site of the mill.

Resuming our walk up the main street, which is margined with several shops and houses, we pause at the brow of the hill. Three sunny cottages, with gardens sloping to the road, will be seen on our right. This is **Orchard Bank,** and it was from one of these houses that an anonymous woman made a desperate bid for freedom during the Plague. She was intercepted at Tideswell, however, and chased back by an angry mob.

The first Methodist sermon was preached in 1765 by Matthew Mayer, of Portwood Hall, near Stockport, who stood against the former smithy and old barn between Orchard Bank and the Royal Oak Hotel. 'The preacher stationed himself by Furness's barnside, but so much hostility was exhibited on this and subsequent occasions that he narrowly escaped with his life. The few friends of the preacher were pelted with brick-bats, mud, stones and other missiles; to such a degree did the infatuated multitude carry their opposition, that the preachers had the ring-leaders brought before the magistrates, who bound them in recognition of their good behaviour in future'. The first Methodist in Eyam appears to have been a certain Joseph Benningson, nicknamed 'Bishop Benson', who had his windows smashed for entertaining Methodist preachers. In the Parish Register is the entry: '1793, *March* 13. *Buried Joseph Bennington, the first that introduced Methodism into Eyam*'.

An interesting record of faith healing at Eyam has been preserved in corres-pondence between two early Methodist ministers, when the Rev. William Bramwell wrote to the Rev. J. Drake as follows:-

'A strange thing happened on the day when I got to Sheffield. At Eyam, a few miles from Sheffield, a poor woman in our Society, who had been quite blind for six years, had her eyes instantly opened, and thanks for this great temporal mercy were offered to God in the public congregation at Sheffield. The manner in which it was effected was a follows: Being very poor, she cried to God that He would be pleased to show her some way by which she might earn bread. He heard her prayer and miraculously opened her eyes, to the wonder of all. Her children ran into the street, crying out, 'Mother can see!' and her house was immediately filled with people, who joined her in thanksgiving. Her eyesight still continues clear. O God, what canst Thou not do!'

Just past the Royal Oak Hotel, a sturdily built house is set well back from the road.

Evidently the architect responsible for its design hesitated as to whether he should create a mansion or a cottage, and seems to have compromised with happy effect. Its mullioned windows are dignified with diamond panes where the smouldering fires of sunset linger. Over the gabled windows are shields carved with emblems of heraldry—a *bend* and a *chevron*—which do not appear to have any relationship with a family crest. The initials and date R.F. 1615 are carved over the door as an enduring monument to its builder.

The very stones of this house are steeped in history! Within its walls early stalwarts of nonconformity were persecuted; a poet was born and spent his boyhood beneath its roof; and many a Christmas-card scene must have enlivened this yard when it was the terminus for horse-drawn coaches plying between Eyam and Sheffield. The large building on the left, with its arched entrance, was the coach-house.

From an early publication entitled *Abstract of the Sufferings of people called Quakers from 1660 to 1666*, we gather that an ancestor of the poet occupied the house at this period. This Richard Furness was an early convert to the faith of George Fox, and suffered distraint to the value of 3s. 4d. because he refused to pay Steeplehouse rates assessed at 1s. 4d. He was later deprived of goods valued at £1 6s. 8d. for the offence of not paying 5d. levied for Easter offerings! The climax was reached on April 23rd, 1661, when a Quaker meeting was rudely interrupted by the village constable and several soldiers. During the skirmish which ensued, Elizabeth Deane was roughly handled whilst in the act of prayer, being dragged outside, 'and shamefully tearing her clothes, not suffering her to get on her feet. With like violence they pulled out the Rest, some by the Hair of the Head, others by the Legs, and with their Heads on the Ground'.

They were kept all night in a barn, then taken the next day to Crich where they spent the night in a room, many of them lying on the floor, without even a little straw. There were thirty-one men and ten women. Two of the men were committed to the House of Correction and were "put into a close Hole, where they could not stand upright, nor could they have liberty to come out to ease their Bodies, but most do it in the place. Their Books and Letters were taken away and not restored again; and when in that straight confinement they were praying to the Lord, their Keeper, in a rage, would come and strike them in the face and attempt to stop their mouths! Nor were their Friends permitted to visit or relieve them'.

On August 2nd, 1791, Samuel and Margaret Furness rejoiced at the gift of a son—one of their family of seven sons and two daughters. Taught by his mother, the future poet could read with ease at the age of four, and was later educated at the village school under the supervision of 'masters who knew how to apply a thick leathern thong to the backs of the boys, of which the poet got his share'. Upon leaving school, Richard was employed as book-keeper for two weaving factories in Eyam, but soon relinquished this position in favour of apprenticeship to a Chesterfield currier. During the war with Napoleon I he became friendly with captive French officers who taught him their language.

At seventeen Richard became converted to Wesleyan Methodism and undertook the responsibilities of the lay ministry. Upon visiting London he was invited to preach before the distinguished Dr. Adam Clarke, and was complimented upon his sermon. Unfortunately, his composition of a patriotic song written to celebrate the defeat of the French in Holland, proved so popular in public-houses that it caused a breach with the Methodists, and resulted in his return to the Established Church.

After many adventures Richard returned to his native village and there launched into business as a currier. Had he shown as much interest in pelts as he did in poetry, he would have undoubtedly prospered, but more of his time was devoted to literature than to leather, and his prospects in business became daily more bleak and cheerless. This ominous position developed at an awkward time for it coincided with his choice of a wife to whom he was able to offer little but struggle, hardship, and the fiery warmth of his affection. At the annual Wakes he had fallen in love with Frances Ibbotson, of Hathersage. This young lady welcomed the ardent overtures of the poet, but her father—a shrewd and prosperous farmer—regarded the courtship with blunt disfavour. Nevertheless, early one morning in 1816, the couple eloped and roused the Rev. J. le Cornu, Vicar of Hathersage, with an urgent request to be married. Pointing out that such a procedure was illegal at that early hour, the Vicar agreed to lock them in church until 8 a.m. when the ceremony was duly performed.

Shortly afterwards the business at Eyam failed, and, after spending four years under the roof of his father-in-law, to whom he had become reconciled, Richard secured an appointment in 1821 as schoolmaster at Dore Free School—a position for which he was well qualified and which he filled with credit and distinction. In 1832 a subscription edition of his poetical works was published and warmly acclaimed in literary circles. He died at Dore on December 13th, 1857, and was buried at his own request ' 'neath those tall trees' in Eyam churchyard where a recently restored monument marks his grave.

Dr. G. C. Holland, his biographer, wrote that 'Eyam and its beauties were strongly impressed upon his heart and he has sung them in lines that succeeding generations will not allow to die. He was a son of the Peak, had breathed its invigorating air and felt its awakening influence. It was the green spot in memory to which he affectionately turned amidst the monotony and vicissitudes of life'. The centenary of the poet's death was fittingly commemorated at Eyam with a meeting at which his poems were recited, and several of the Christmas carols he had written and for which he composed the music, were sung by the local choirs. Biographical tributes were paid and a muffled peal rung on the church bells. A further mark of esteem was a wells-dressing tableau dedicated to his memory.

Passing the next house and turning up a short lane, we are confronted with a farmyard gate to the left of which is a stile. Our path lies through the farmyard and between farm buildings until we reach a second gate and stile. But, before proceeding, let us notice the old farmhouse on our left. This is known as **Hollins' House.**

It may be pointed out that the date-stone over the door is not a reliable indication of the age of the house, but probably denoted the year of its enlargement or reconstruction. It may have been from this house that stout-hearted Christopher Merril—his arquebus over his shoulder—set out in 1585 in company with Thomas Townsende, Edmunde Wilson and Nycholas Redferne to be 'trayned at Backwell' under Sir John Manners and Robert Eyre, Esq., for the defence of their country against the threatened Spanish invasion. How the curious villagers must have gathered round these men who had been conscripted for war. These men with the mud of the fallow field, or the clay of the lead-mine, clinging to their boots. They were more familiar with the friendly warmth of the flail, or the handle of a pick, than with the cold steel of swords and muskets. Yet it had been ordained that they should exchange the peace of the harvest-field for the tumult and confusion of the battle-field! Incidentally, the firearms and armoury then afforded by the village amounted to one caliver, one corselet, one arquebus and one bill!

Two years later, Christopher was recalled for military service, although the surname appears on the muster roll as Merrell—probably due to a clerical error or to the indifference shown in those days towards correct spelling. About eighty years afterwards, Andrew Merrill locked the door of his house and set out under far different circumstances. Instead of a firearm he carried a few personal belongings. And instead of candidates for military honour he was accompanied by a cockerel which shared his lonely exile in a moorland hut until the plague had spent its fury.

A less fortunate occupant of the farmhouse was Humphrey Merrill, whose grave lies in the field through which passes a public footpath. The tomb lies in a hollow of this field, but is on private land. It is a lonely tomb! Nature has surrounded it with simple meadow flowers and its stones are anointed with tears of dew and rain. Children scramble over it and cows have worn the stone slab with rubbing against it. Nor has any moralist ventured to inscribe it with some dreary epitaph. Just the initials H.M. and the date 1666 at the end . . . The friendly flowers still keep it company; the cows still soothe themselves against its polished masonry; the feet of children climb over it with innocent irreverence and we wonder if this farmer of plague days loved the flowers, his cattle, and the children playing in the meadows?

A little further up the main street, Tideswell Lane turns abruptly to the left and, at the point where it curves to the right is a cottage on the left which tradition claims was the home of Marshall Howe, sexton of the plague days. Also further up the street, on the left side, is a printing works which was originally Wain's silk factory and then became a shoe factory.

Retracing our steps and taking the Hawkhill Road, we pass the former village almshouses, and see Mompesson's Well (a distance of over one mile)—passing the graves of two sisters—the Bull Ring—Lydgate Graves—and Riley Graves (over half a mile).

Having returned to the road junction near Bradshaw Hall, we turn left up the hill past the Methodist Church. As will be seen from the sketch map, we have the choice of several routes to Mompesson's Well, but this is the only one available to the motorist and also affords a more gradual climb to the pedestrian.

The road soon turns sharply and steeply to the right, but, before proceeding, we notice the old bridle-way bearing a little to the left. This winds up the steep hillside and joins the Occupation Road (built to provide employment during a period of industrial recession) near a group of farm buildings. Just beyond at the next bend are three houses commanding magnificent views. One of these was formerly occupied by R. Murray Gilchrist, the Victorian novelist, and Eyam frequently figures in his novels and short stories as *Milton*. Here is his description of a Dickensian scene in the forecourt of Richard Furness's birthplace when preparations were being made for a journey by road to Sheffield. 'All the way they could see Cowper's yard, where the old-fashioned yellow omnibus stood piled with hampers, ready for the three flea-bitten horses to be led from the stable . . . The three women occupied the seat behind the driver; at their back, covered with a sheet of tarpaulin, was a crate of week-old ducklings, incubator-hatched for the Malton market; beyond this were egg and butter baskets, and hampers of trussed fowls. Some time was passed in the yard, where Cowper's son strutted, lustily crowing through a green-rusted brass horn, to warn all would-be passengers that starting time was near . . . "

Having made this digression in thought, *we continue along the road and observe a pleasantly situated house standing back from the road on our left.* Until it was restored and extended, it had mock battlements which denoted that it was the village poorhouse. At one time there were three small houses occupied by widows. It is quite likely that they were once equipped with looms for the employment of the inmates, but unfortunately the Overseer's of the Poor Accounts are missing, or these would supply information concerning this former village institution. At this pleasant spot, the decrepit and infirm; the distressed and feeble-minded; the victims of ill-health and misfortune spent their declining days. Pain, misery and humiliation seem to have been the lot of those who reluctantly sought the shelter of the poorhouse, and many of the occupants bitterly resented the fact that life's pilgrimage had brought them to this inglorious shrine. No one envied them . . . few pitied them. They were the paupers of the parish . . . parasites . . . outcasts of rural society!

William Wood referred to several plague memorials near this place. 'Behind, or rather at the west end of some dwellings, once known as the Poor-houses, one or two of these stones, which are said to have recorded the deaths of some persons of the name of Whiteley, have been of late demolished'.

A little further along on our left we notice a drive which steeply ascends to Beech Hurst, a large substantial house which is now a youth hostel. It was built during the first decade of the present century by the late William Nixon and is surmounted by an imposing turret from which there is a magnificent view of the

Old Steam Wagon at Cupola Works, 1912. *Courtesy of Glebe Mines Limited.*

Surface Operations at Glebe Mines, 1897.
Courtesy of Glebe Mines Limited.

Underground Operations at Ladywash Mine, 1965.
Courtesy of Glebe Mines Limited.

34

surrounding countryside. Over the entrance to the house is carved the early Christian salutation, 'Peace be unto this house', reminding us that Mr. Nixon was a lay preacher. He was also a member of the Bakewell bench of magistrates and is remembered travelling to that town with his carriage and coachman.

About half a mile beyond, we reach a road junction opposite a shallow pool. Ignoring the road branching to the left, we proceed about fifty yards further and find **Mompesson's Well** *in a cul-de-sac sloping away to our left.*

This well, which has been enclosed with iron railings as a precaution against vandalism, was the scene of one of the strangest markets in history, for provisions were brought here during the Plague and coins left for payment had to be cleansed in the water bubbling from this spring.

From here we see the chimney and headframe of the rehabilitated Ladywash Mine, one of the last mines sunk to penetrate the Edgeside Vein which dips steeply at this point towards the water table. Forming a background to Lady-wash Mine can be seen the summit of Sir William Hill with the slender filigree framework of two police radio masts pointing towards the sky.

Returning along the road by which we came, we notice, about halfway back to the village, a narrow gate and stile on our left. At this point, incidentally, we stand exactly 1,000 *ft. above sea level. Through the stile we take the path descending obliquely across a hillocky field to a lane leading down into the village.* Near this field is the site of two horizontal gravestones inscribed **Margaret Teylor 1666** and **Alies Teylor 1666.** For over three centuries they have lain unmolested upon this sunny hillside near the long vanished home of the two sisters, but in latter years the stones have been turfed over to conceal their location and the visitor seeks them in vain.

Upon re-entering the village, the road soon divides to encircle a group of houses before opening into the Square. Just across from the Forester's House—a former inn—may be seen the **Bull Ring.** The small cover protecting the ring may be easily raised to facilitate inspection. After the practice of baiting bulls had been abolished the ring became buried beneath a crust of road-repairing material for many years and was uncovered in 1911. Further layers of surfacing material made it necessary to excavate the boulder to which it is attached and it was elevated to its present level in 1965.

Crossing the Square we ascend the lane known as the Lidgett or Lydgate—a place recalling the gate which sealed off the village during the hours of darkness in olden days. A rota of able-bodied men took turns to preserve the security of the village by keeping watch and ward here. Armed with a halberd, it was the duty of the sentry to challenge strangers seeking admission to the village from dusk to dawn.

On the right side of the road we see Lydgate House where William Wood, the village historian, was born and spent much of his life. Wood's father was a lead-miner, owning the cottage in which he lived and renting a couple of fields for the support of a cow. He played the hautboy in the Church choir. William was the second of his family of four sons and three daughters, and was born on December 6th, 1804. His only source of education was that provided by the Sunday School of which his father was superintendent. To improve his knowledge, he frequently walked several miles to borrow books, and also purchased a copy of Cobbett's 'grammar' which he attached to his hand-loom in order to combine his studies with the duties of his daily occupation. This was the secret of his extensive vocabulary.

When William was about twenty years of age, a subscription library was established in Eyam, providing a wider range of literature, and he became one of its most regular patrons and eventually its secretary. He also joined an essay and debating society attached to the library, and this gave scope for the development of his gifts of writing and rhetoric. He was encouraged to contribute both poetry and articles to local journals. Music was another interest, and, like his father, he was an instrumentalist in the church choir, and also organised and instructed a village band. His first literary venture, *Genius of the Peak and other Poems* appeared in 1837. Five years later his most popular work, *The History and Antiquities of Eyam*, was published by subscription. A second edition was printed in 1848, and this was enlarged in 1860. Two years later his collection of legends and stories, *Tales and Traditions of the Peak* was published. Wood died on June 27th, 1865, and was buried near the Church where a small headstone bearing his initials and date of death identifies his grave. A short distance away a large monument was erected by subscription, and is often mistaken for his actual grave.

A little further on our right we find an enclosure containing two lichened stones and formerly a weeping ash with its branches sadly twisted and deformed. These are known as the **Lydgate Graves.** It is a place unconsecrated by any ecclesiastical ritual, yet sacred to the memory of a father and daughter of whom the inscriptions quaintly say. '*Here lye buried George Darby, who dyed July 4th, 1666; Mary the daughter of George Darby, dyed September 4th, 1666.*

Anyone wishing to visit all the sites connected with the Plague may wish to see an indented boulder on the Cliff between Eyam and Stoney Middleton. This is about half a mile out of the village, and to reach it we continue up the lane to the stile between two gates. Passing through the stile and crossing two fields, the path is then hemmed in by two stone walls, and leads us to a large pasture field. The path continues through the middle of this field and to the left we see a circle of trees. Midway between the path and the trees we find the **Boundary Stone,** *a large sand-stone boulder which may be an erratic left in glacial times. The holes drilled in the surface are said to have been filled with vinegar for the disinfection of coins as at Mompesson's Well. R. M. Gilchrist says: 'Beside the field path that descends to Stoney Middleton, where the wild gilliflowers grow, an old fellow once showed me a flat stone in which were cut several round holes. There, said he, the Eyam folk had dropped their coins in vinegar for disinfecting purposes, and the inhabitants of the surrounding country had exchanged them for provisions'.*

Returning to the village we re-enter the Square, turn right and follow the main road to the housing estate at the eastern limit of the village. Reaching the houses on the fringe of the estate, we bear left up the road through the wood. Just over the brow of the hill we see **Riley Graves** *in the field on our left.*

Here a woman was condemned to a life of loneliness and sorrow.

The Talbots of Riley suffered extinction during the July of 1666, but the earth was still hungry and the locust of plague passed on to the farm of John Hancock. With one exception, the whole family died within the space of a week and it was the mother who was spared to fill the mournful office of sexton! People living across the valley at Stoney Middleton are said to have watched Mrs. Hancock digging graves and dragging the bodies from her home to the place of interment. Stricken with grief, the poor woman escaped to Sheffield where she lived with her only surviving son, who was an apprentice in the silver trade.

Ebenezer Rhodes wrote: 'About the year 1750, a Mr. Joseph Hancock, a descendant of this family, discovered, or rather *recovered*, the art of covering ingots of copper with plate silver, which were afterwards flattened under rollers, and manufactured into a variety of articles in imitation of wrought silver plate . . . I have not hesitated to use the term recovered, as applicable to the art of which Mr. Joseph Hancock has been considered the founder, for I am well aware that the practice of covering one metal with another more precious is of great antiquity. That articles plated with silver, particularly candlesticks, were in use during the reign of Henry the Seventh, can hardly admit of controversy . . .' The above claim is also made for a Mr. Thomas Bolsover, of Whiteley Wood, who formed the idea while mending a knife and applied the method to buttons and buckles, while Hancock, a brazier, realised the wider application to cutlery, candlesticks and other Sheffield Plate ware.

The inscription and epitaph on the father's tomb reads:-

John Hancock, sen., Buried August 7, 1666.

> Remember man
> As thou go'st by,
> As thou art now,
> Even once was I;
> As I doe now
> So must thou lie,
> Remember man
> That thou must die.

Elizabeth Hancock, Buried Aug. 3, 1666.
John Hancock, Buried Aug. 3, 1666.
Oner Hancock, Buried Aug. 7, 1666.
William Hancock, Buried Aug. 7, 1666.
Alice Hancock, Buried Aug. 9, 1666.
Ann Hancock, Buried Aug. 10, 1666.

The tomb of the father marks his actual grave, but the other stones were assembled from their respective sites and erected in this enclosure by Thomas Birds, an Eyam antiquary, and at a later date the inscriptions were cut more deeply at the expense of Sir Henry Burford Hancock, Governor General of Gibraltar.

Following the flight of Mrs. Hancock, the tenantless farm crumbled into such a state of ruin that it was pulled down. The site can still be distinguished by a terrace on the hillside in the direction of the present Riley House Farm.

The present farmhouse, where the Talbots lived, was re-built during the last century, but the tabular monument inscribed *Richard Talbot, Catherine his wife, two sons and three daughters, buried July*, 1666, still exists in the orchard.

As we stand in this graveyard hallowed by tragic memories, we may recall some of the pilgrims who have visited this simple but impressive shrine, where the lark sings in the sky and sheep nibble the tender grass. Among them are men who have enriched local and national literature with the wealth of their words. Spencer T. Hall, Ebenezer Rhodes, William and Mary Howitt, Ebenezer Elliott, Arthur Mee, H. V. Morton and many others, and it may be fitting to close this literary tour of Eyam with Dr. S. T. Hall's description of the scene commanded from this spot.

'Before me were hundreds of green fields, sloping beautifully down from Longstone Edge to Middleton Dale, which was folded up almost out of sight in the pastoral country beneath me; and, from the hidden limekilns there, arose light films of smoke, like moving wreaths of evening mist. On the other hand lay Eyam village, with its old grey tower and rustic roofs, reposing among the trees . . . In one place a tall windmill was slowly flinging round its long dark sails in the air, as constantly as if it were set to count the strides of Time; in another stood some solitary cottage on the lea, its windows flashing back the bright rays of the descending sun.

'Here at hand was a substantial farm-house, around which stood garners and ricks, and tall sheltering trees, and flocks and herds about its gate. There, afar off, diminished by the distance to a little cluster, was a mountain hamlet, bleak, hoary, and cold, as though it had never known the luxury of a summer smile.

'Anon sank the sun behind a western cloud, between which and one still lower there was a dazzling opening, and through it streamed the light, silent and swift over the grassy hills, giving a momentary brilliancy to every object in turn and then again leaving all things more dim and indistinct than before'.

An account of the Plague

And many are the pilgrim feet which tread
Its rocky steeps; which thither yearly go:
Yet less by love of Nature's wonders led,
Than by the memory of a mighty woe,
Which smote, like blasting thunder, long ago,
The peopled hills . . .

(WILLIAM AND MARY HOWITT)

Early Plagues   A thousand years before bubonic plague struck London in 1664, Britain was in the throes of a similar epidemic. It invaded castle and cottage, mansion and monastery, priory and palace, farmhouse bothie and fisherman's booth, to carry away both the poor and the privileged, the sick and the healthy, the weak and the strong. During the year 664 the Bishop of Northumbria died of plague, as did St. Cedd at Lastingham; while the King of Kent and the Archbishop of Canterbury both died on the same day that year. Boisil, the saintly prior of Melrose, was another victim of that period. And down through the intervening centuries, such outbreaks brought periods of suffering and sorrow to the population of hamlet and village, town and city.

Causes of Plague   The frequency of epidemics in past days was largely due to insanitation. In the cities and towns people were herded together in a congestion of ill-planned houses intersected by narrow and sunless streets. Systems of drainage were also inadequate or non-existent, and household refuse was often emptied into the streets and left to fester with other filth in open gutters—fit breeding places for germs of disease.

For centuries the medical profession was baffled as to the cause of plague. Domestic pets were slaughtered on several occasions because they were suspected of carrying infection. Sailors, too, were accused of bringing the disease from Oriental countries where plague was indigenous, because outbreaks often occurred at ports. In 1894, however, the bacillus of plague was identified, and it was later discovered that the microbes were actually carried by rat-fleas. Soon it was conclusively proved that the black (house) rats which infested ships, warehouses, dockside buildings and nearby dwellings, were guilty of spreading the disease in the first instance. Towards the close of the 17th century this species was almost exterminated by the rapid multiplication of brown (sewer) rats, which, although capable of carrying the infection, are much more timid and shy of human company.

Bubonic or Glandular Plague acquired its name from the carbuncles or tumours which affected the victim's glands. These were called buboes. The bacillus

39

(plague germ) invaded the body by tiny punctures in the skin caused by the flea-bites and spread by way of lymphatics in the blood stream to the glandular parts of the body which became painfully inflamed. These swellings at the neck, groin and armpits, sometimes developed within twelve to fourteen hours. Infection was attended by the symptoms of shivering, sickness, headache, inflammation of the lungs and delirium. Recovery was sometimes possible if the patient could be induced to vomit and sweating antidotes were also applied, but if the 'macula'—a purple blemish—appeared on the chest of the victim, then death was inevitable. This dreaded 'token' appeared as a livid blotch on the skin and was due to the haemorrhagic manifestation of the disease. Another symptom was the uncontrollable rolling of the eyeballs.

The disease was sometimes recognised, as in the case of Mrs. Katherine Mompesson, by an imagined sweetness of the air due to an increase in the patient's blood temperature. This may have been why an eminent London apothecary propounded the theory that plague was of miasmatic origin, contending that it was caused by chemical exhalations, or other poisonous fumes and noxious odours, rising out of mines, marshes and underground workings. At the time of the Black Death—so named because of the black spots which discoloured the skin, and sometimes confused with bubonic plague—old writers reported earthquakes, atmospheric pollution, 'thick stinking mists' and a pestiferous wind which struck people in the streets to die writhing in agony.

It was possible to contract infection from the cough of a victim suffering from plague pneumonia, or even as the result of a slight graze caused by a scratch from infected material such as linen or cloth. And, incidentally, it has been proved that the germs will exist for months at a medium temperature in dry cloth. Woollen goods were particularly treacherous, nursing the bacilli and encouraging gestation. Six soldiers died at Constantinople after successively wearing the tunic of a comrade dead of the plague. A feather mattress became the death-bed of many who slept upon it. Some children in Holland died after playing on clothes brought from an infected house in another locality. Infected bandages, which had been stuffed between the wainscot and wall of a house in Paris, were found *many years afterwards* and caused a serious epidemic in the city. Reference will later be made to an alleged revival of the plague in Eyam after buried clothing had been dug up nearly a century after the Plague.

There is a tradition in Canterbury that the cloth which acted as carrier of the Eyam plague was woven on the looms of weavers in that city.

It is interesting to note that the prevalence of plague was reflected in industrial legislation made in 1666 to encourage the wool trade, for the *Burial in Woollen Act* of that year stated 'No corpse of any person (except those who shall die of the plague) shall be buried in any shift, sheet, or shroud or anything made or mingled with flax, hemp, silk, hair, gold or silver or in any stuff or anything, other than what is made of sheep's wool only . . . or be put into any coffin or faced with any other material but sheep's wool only.' It is also interesting to find that fear of the plague has been woven into the texture of London's traditions, as in the annual disinfecting of the Guildhall with sweet herbs preparatory to the election of the Lord Mayor on Michaelmas Day.

Few people would perhaps associate this awful disease with an innocent nursery rhyme, yet the familiar jingle, 'Ring a ring o' roses', is descriptive of the plague and its effects. The ring of roses was the purple rash or plague spot; the pocket full of posies the pomanders of herbs or nosegays thought to prevent the inhalation of the plague and used as disinfectants; the sneezing—'atishoo, atishoo'—symptoms resembling a chill; and the fatal and final phase of the illness was signified by 'we all fall down.'

Recipes against the Plague   Treatment of the disease was largely exploratory and experimental due to the prevailing ignorance of its causes.

The register of East Retford Church contains a quaint prescription to ward off the plague, and was entered by Thomas Gylby, vicar from 1701 to 1751, and copied by his successor, Joshua Sampson (1752-1772). 'In ye time of a plague let the person either infected or fearfull of ye infection, take a pennyworth of Dragon water, a pennyworth of oyle Olive, Mithrodite 1d. and treacle 1d., then take an unyon and fill it full of pepper, w'n you have fcraped it, then roaft it and after that put in to ye liquor and ftrain and drink it in ye morning, and if you take ye same at night lay foap and bay falt to your feet, and fweat upon it and with God's blesfing you fhall recover.'

The Plagues Approved Physitian counselled 'If there doe a botch appear; take a Pigeon and pluke the feathers off her tail, very bare, and set her tail to the sore, and shee will draw out the venome till shee die; then take another set too likewise, continuing so till all the venome be drawne out which you shall see by the Pigeons, for they will die with the venome as long as there is any in: also a chicken or henn is very good . . All should studiously avoid dancing, running, leaping about, lechery and bathing.'

The remedy approved by the College of Physicians was :- 'Take a greate onion, hollow it, put in a fig one cut small and a dram of Venice treacle; put it close stopt in wet paper, and roast it in the embers; apply it hot into the tumour, lay three or four, one after another; let one lie three hours.'

William Boghurst, an apothecary, applied the following remedy to a female patient. 'I laid a great Mastiff Puppy Dog upon her breasts two or three hours together, and made her drink Dill, Pennyroyal, Fennell and Aniseed Water, for she was a fat woman and could bear it.' Another remedy recommended to sufferers in London was:- 'Let everyone take every morning a little London treacle, or the kernel of a walnut, with five leaves of rue and a grain of salt beaten together and roasted in a fig, and so eaten.' Garlick is said to have been the chief herbal ingredient in a potion known as 'thieves' vinegar' which was drunk by the ghoulish people who haunted the streets of London and looted the contents of deserted pest-houses. Ivy berries were also used with considerable success in London and it was found that they possessed alexiphermic and sudorific values.

A Derbyshire family had the following royal prescription:- 'A preservative from the Kings Matie against the Plague. Take Redd Sage, herbe of grasse, Elder leaves and bramble leaves of either (each) one handfull. Strayne them with a quarte of whyte wyne, drynke hereof a spoonfull everye morninge for nyne days togeather and the firste spoonfull will preserve you for twenty-four dayes, and see the nynth spoonfull will suffice for the whole year. If the ptie be infected then take with the thing aforesaid Scabious water and Betany water and a little of the best Treakell and it shall, by the grace of God, dryve oute all the venome from the hurte but yf the Botche appeare then take a handfull of Red sagge, Elder leaves, bramble leaves, mustery seed and beate them all together and make thereof a plaster.'

'Plague water' was another sovereign remedy kept as a precaution against infection. This consisted of a compound of a pound each of twenty roots, sixteen flowers, nineteen seeds, together with an ounce each of nutmeg, cloves and mace. The method was to shred the flowers, bruise the berries and pound the roots and spices. A peck of green walnuts was then added and, after all the ingredients had been mixed together, the concoction was steeped in wine lees and had to be distilled a week later.

John Wesley collected recipes for the prevention and also the cure of plague as follows:- (To prevent) 'Eat Marigold Flowers daily, as a sallad, with Oil and Vinegar; or, A little of the tops of Rue with bread and butter, every morning; or Infuse Rue, Sage, Mint, Rosemary, Wormwood, of each a handful, in two quarts of the sharpest Vinegar, over warm embers for eight days. Then strain it through a flannel and add half an ounce of Camphire, dissolved in three ounces of rectified Spirits of Wine. With this wash the Loins, Face and Mouth, and snuff a little up the nose when you go abroad, Smell to a spunge dipt therein, when you approach infected persons or places'. (To cure). 'Cold water alone, drank largely, has cured it: or, An ounce or two of the juice of Marigolds; or, Take a dram of Angelica powder'd every six hours. It is a strong sweat; or, After bleeding fifty or sixty ounces, drink very largely of water sharpened with Spirit of Vitriol; or, A draught of Brine as soon as seized; sweat in bed, take not other drinks for some hours; or, Use Lemon-juice largely with every thing.'

Another attempted means of warding off infection was by the use of plague-pans. These are like miniature warming-pans which they resemble in detail, except that the lids are perforated. Aromatic herbs were heated in these pans and the scent diffused through the vents to act as an equivalent to the modern aerosol. Pomanders served a similar, but more convenient, purpose and were carried about by persons passing through areas of infection.

A 20th Century Re-appraisal   It is worthy of note that, in the light of discoveries made during the years which have intervened since 1665-66, a new school of thought and philosophy has evolved a re-evaluation of the story of the Plague. This has been developed from a clinical and quite dispassionate examination of facts revealed by the researches of modern medical science. Discarding the rose-tinted spectacles of sentiment and melodrama, those who have pursued this line of enquiry have based their conclusions on the evidence of microscope and test tube. And while they have doubtless found this a stimulating and refreshing exercise, and one which has value in the field of historical criticism, we fear that their findings may offend those who favour the claims of popular and conventional history. Nor should such revelations be allowed to impeach or impair the reputation of Mompesson and Stanley by any suggestion that they were prompted by motives of self-seeking or personal aggrandizement.

Impartial investigation has adduced the theory that men like Mompesson and Stanley, and the Lord Mayor of London (Sir John Lawrence) and his Court of

Aldermen, were misguided in counselling villagers or compelling citizens to repress the instincts of self-preservation and remain in quarantine, because of the current misunderstanding of this particular disease. Compulsory isolation was often insisted upon both for the victims and their contacts, whereas it is now hypothetically argued that unrestrained flight might have spared much misery and loss of life, and without undue risk of exposing others to infection. But we must ever remember that Mompesson and Stanley were prompted by a genuine concern for the safety of people outside Eyam and acted according to contemporary knowledge, and therefore are to be commended for their courage and not condemned for their lack of knowledge.

Methods of treatment are now known to have been mistaken owing to the belief that plague was a glandular fever and contagious in whatever form it was manifested. It is also known that carrying posies of herbs and civet boxes, and washing coins in a solution of vinegar and water for purposes of sterilization, were needless precautions. It is also now known that handling paper or parchment was not an infection risk. Mompesson had his letter to John Beilby transcribed by a friend at Stoney Middleton, being 'loath to affright you with a paper from my hands', while his letter to Sir George Saville was dictated upon Eyam Moor to the Rev. John Walker, Vicar of Hathersage, who added a postscript to reassure the recipient that he was in no danger of infection.

Although people shrank from any contact with a plague victim, they did not realise that the glandular inflammation was non-infectious to the touch. They were equally unaware that a person suffering from pneumonic plague was inadvertently spraying bacteria during bouts of coughing and sneezing; a fact which gives point to the proverb that 'coughs and sneezes spread diseases'. Another unrecognised manifestation was the septicemic poisoning of the blood stream, and again the role of the rat and bacilli-carrying rat-flea was unsuspected in the spread of the disease. The discovery and application of sulfa drugs for use in the treatment of plague has done much to militate against its lethal effects, together with education in personal and public hygiene, improvements in domestic sanitation, and other health reforms of recent years.

But let us not be so blinded by the light of these retrospective researches that we forget the darkness of the 17th century, and let us bear in mind that we are thinking of the predicament of people in a remote Peakland parish, without doctor or drug dispensary, and without the crude hospital services of their day. And if our judgment of their actions is still perverted, let us contrast the courage of the two Eyam clergymen with the craven cowardice of a contemporary rector placed in a similar situation and confronted with the same challenge.

The Sad Story of Vernham Dene   The Hampshire village of Vernham Dene has a similar but even sadder story than that of Eyam, for the rector of that parish failed to measure up to the standard of heroism required by such a crisis. About the same time that plague was pruning out the population of Eyam, the same disease was devastating Vernham Dene. The rector persuaded his stricken parishioners to isolate themselves in a camp near the route of the Roman road known as Chute Causeway, promising to supply them with the victuals and medicines they needed. But fear of infection overwhelmed him in his intention to perform the self-assigned task, and the wretched sufferers were left to perish of pestilence or starvation! But his cowardly neglect did not spare him from sharing the fate he feared and he was numbered with the victims. Tradition tells that his disconsolate ghost is sometimes seen climbing the steep hill towards the site of the camp—perhaps filled with remorse and anxious to seek expiation for the sin of failing to keep faith with his flock!

Notable Plagues During the years 1346-51 it is estimated that 25,000,000 people died in Europe of the Black Death, and that a similar number perished in the Far East. In China the death roll reached millions. Great numbers also died in India. Half the population of Italy was mown down in the black harvest, and whole village communities suffered extinction in France. Over a quarter of the population of England died within this period! Although there had been minor outbreaks of plague in this country before the Black Death had crept across the Continent, it was during this fateful period that rats were first introduced into England. They came as passengers in ships from Oriental countries—and they decided to stay!

Two-thirds of the clergy in Derbyshire fell victims to the disease in 1349.

Plague at Curbar During the year 1632 an isolated farm known as Grislow-fields, near Curbar, was suddenly depopulated by plague. Below the crags of Curbar Edge five slabs of roughly hewn stone lying in a marshy hollow are inscribed with the initials T.C. 1632., A.C., O.C., N.C. and T.C. to remind us that Thomas Cundy, his wife, Ada, and their three children—Olive, Nellie and Thomas—were among the victims. Some years ago the site of the graves was more clearly identified by a memorial stone erected at the instigation of the late Lady Finch of Curbar, her husband, Sir Ernest, Mr. G. Goddard, then chairman of the Parish Council, Mr. E. Askey (Clerk) and other interested residents. The author of this work was invited to speak at a ceremony arranged by the Parish Council and conducted by the Vicar the Rev. G. F. Cooke, to mark this event.

During this visitation of 1632 several homes were visited in Curbar and it is known that a family named Sheldon and others suffered bereavement. Unfortunately the hamlet had no chronicler to record this phase of its otherwise uneventful history. William Wood has a few comments on the event and the Rev. James Cocker, a native of nearby Calver, who went as a missionary to New Zealand, tells of the Cundys in his *Blossomby Idylls*.

For many years a tradition had lingered in the village that Willoughby's (or Worrall's) Orchard below the Wesleyan Reform Chapel was the site of a communal grave where victims had been buried. Bones were also dug up in the orchard. Then the tradition was rather dramatically confirmed in 1967 when Mr. J. Hallam was making a garden for the house he had built on this site. Upon removing the turf, he uncovered a long irregular slab of gritstone with the initials I. or J.C. and the date 1632, and thus supplied some measure of proof for William Wood's statement that a family named Cooke or Clarke had been among the victims. Several other stones were thought to have been located by probing with an iron rod, but were left undisturbed beneath the surface.

Residents of Curbar would normally have been buried at Baslow in which parish the hamlet was incorporated in those days, but it was obviously considered expedient to inter the victims as quickly and quietly and as near to their homes as possible.

During September, 1975, the author was notified that a further grave had been accidentally exposed about two hundred yards higher than the Cundy group. The turf which had covered the stone appeared to have been kicked away by horses climbing the pony-trekking path which skirts the situation of the grave. Bearing the initials and date H.W. 1632, this stone has been squared and carefully dressed to a regular shape. The figure 3 is carved in reverse; a curious feature which is also to be noted in the inscription on the grave in Mr. Hallam's garden. The stone slopes slightly with the natural configuration of the ground, and is at the edge of a fairly level area which was probably the site of a dwelling-house before the enclosure of the moor. It is hardly likely that victims would be carried so far from the village, and there is evidence that a number of houses were formerly situated at a higher level.

Outbreaks at Derby   Derby had several visitations. There were outbreaks in 1586, 1592, 1636 and 1665. The following record concerns that of 1592-93:- '1593. The plague of pestilence by the great goodness and mercy of Almighty God, stay'd past all expectac'on of man, for it rested upon assondayne at what tyme it was dispersed in every corner of the whole p'she; ther was only two houses free from ytt, and yet the Lord bade his angell staye as in David's tyme: His name be blessed for ytt.'

Concerning the 1665 outbreak it is recorded:- 'The town was forsaken: the farmers declined the marketplace, and grass grew upon the spot on which the necessaries of life had been sold. To prevent a famine, the inhabitants erected a stone a little way out of town for the purpose of exchange.' The stone mentioned was the Headless Cross which is now in the Arboretum. Money was rinsed in the vinegar-filled hollow of this stone. As a precaution against infection, tradesmen chewed tobacco, while prospective customers were not allowed to handle goods unless they intended to make a purchase. When a transaction was completed, the purchasers placed their money in vessels filled with vinegar. Tanners, shoe-makers, tobacconists and soap-boilers were noticed to be immune from the disease; whether this was purely coincidence or whether it was due to the nature of their employment is not known.

The value of tobacco as a safeguard was widely recognised, and it is recorded that a boy was punished for refusing to smoke. One wonders whether this started the habit in the gentler sex! Bowls of broken clay pipes were also thrown into the plague pits.

St. Alkmund's church register at Derby has an interesting entry concerning longevity:- '1592. November 17. Thomas Ball was buried, who had lived to the age of 110.' Not all the parishioners were as fortunate, for in the same year the entry was made:- 'Incipit pestus pestifera (The Plague began)', followed by 'Margery Cotes died first of the plague, February 2. N.B. Ninety-one died of the plague in this parish'. The following year brought relief. '1593. Octob. 4. Hic desinit pestis pestifera. Sit Deo gratia.' (The dreadful plague terminated. Thanks be to God). Then in 1637 another entry was made:- 'The plague began in Derby this year.'

Plague at Chesterfield   It has been estimated that about 275 people died of plague in Chesterfield between October, 1588, and November, 1589. If this calculation is correct, the number of deaths and period of thirteen months' duration of the epidemic, corresponds exactly with the figures at Eyam. Following the obituary of Margaret, wife of Francis Cade, and John, her son, on October 2nd., 1586, is the note in the parish register:- 'Here began the great plague of Chesterfield.' At Calow three sisters were buried from one house on a day in July, 1587. Towards the end of the Plague, the baby daughter of John Woodward was given the rather pathetic name of Hope. Her father later became an alderman of the town. The town was again visited in 1608-09.

Nearby Brimington was affected in 1603, and the place-name 'Cabin Fields' recalls the site of the isolation huts built for the accommodation of the victims. Six years later, a Rev. W. Townsend of Holmesfield, died of plague at Brimington. Plague graves are recorded in the parish of Ashover, near Chesterfield, and twenty-six skeletons were found when a tennis court was being made at Overton Hall in 1887. The bodies lay only a few inches below the turf and appeared to have been buried indiscriminately and in haste, and probably with little or no clothing, for no relics were found to help in establishing the period of death. This suggests the probability that they were victims of plague. At Ashover Hay, a few miles away, a field is pointed out where spring patterns the shape of graves with daffodils. Although no stones memorialise the event, these Lenten lilies keep alive the shreds of an otherwise forgotten story of plague!

Ashbourne visited in 1605   The Harl. M.S., 663, contains a list of 24 infected houses and list of 62 victims 'Dead of ye plague in Ashbourne, 1605.' Here are some extracts:-

> 'Brownlow's widow and 3 children,
> Goodin and 2 children, 1 in ye Cabins,
> Chr. Watson's man,
> John Sadler, his wife, a child, his maid,
> Widow Fletcher,
> Widowe Hartill's children,
> Webster's maide, Both in ye coate,
> Olde Tofte,
> Jasper Joyner, a pore wench (quere),
> Joane Wood's boy,
> 2 of Gunner's girles,
> a bastard of Mary Benstone's,
> Mary Benstone herself,
> Rob Phillip's sonne Willm,
> Rob Phillip's youngest girle, May 26,
> Lyon's wive's girle, June 8, from Dove-house green,
> Wm. Robert's girle, June 17.

The Gunner charged Hawley to conceile his boye's sickness and keep him in ye toune till his boile was almost white 3 weeks or thereaboute.'

Belper and Darley Dale visited   The plague laid seige to Belper in 1603 when, out of a population of less than 200, there were 53 victims between the first day of

March and the last of September. In the Darley Dale register for 1551 is the record that 'nine persons were buried from the 5th of Julye till the 10th which dyed of ye sweatinge sicknesse.'

The register at Hope records an outbreak which, although not bubonic plague, appears to have been a disease of a highly contagious nature. In the 'yeare of our Lord God one thousand six hundredth thirtie and six, beganne the great death of many children and others by a contagious desease called the children pocke: and Purple Pocke: and whyt hives with blisters.' 'Hives', according to a definition in the *English Dialect Dictionary*, consists of 'an eruption of the skin, water blebs or blisters . . . a feverish complaint among children.'

The Bride of Wreighill   It was during the fateful year of 1665 that a parcel was on its way from London to the remote village of Wreighill in the county of Durham. It contained a dress length intended for the wedding of a certain Miss Hardyside, but she became the bride of Death and was the first of many victims in that village. Nearly all the inhabitants died and were buried deeply in communal graves where it was thought the remains would never be molested. But not so, for many years later, quantities of bones were unearthed by quarrymen obtaining limestone for burning in their kilns; a grim reminder of an episode in the history of this village which never really recovered from that savage onslaught. For it was recorded that 'Wreighill, about a mile west of Caistron, was once a considerable village, but now consists of cattle folds and a solitary dwelling. In 1816 there were twenty-eight persons living at Wreighill; at the present (1906) there are only four . . . ' It is quite likely that Marjorie Bowen had this story in mind when she wrote *God and the Wedding Dress*, a novel based on Eyam Plague.

Plague at Birmingham   Plague came to Birmingham in the same year, and in the same way, that it came to Eyam. 'The next happening of any great moment was the outbreak of the plague in 1665, which was said to have been brought to the town in a box of clothes by a carrier, which he deposited at the White Hart Inn. The visitation seems to have been a severe one, for it was found impossible to inter the victims in the usual burying-ground, and a full acre of land was set aside at Lady Wood Green (known for many years as the "pest ground") for the reception of those who died of the plague.'

And in Cornwall   Textile goods appear to have been largely responsible for scattering the seeds of infection in remote parts of the country where often the grim harvest of death ripened to maturity.

At Bodmin, Cornwall, the story is told of travelling packmen arriving in the town with stocks of rich velvet, silk and brocade gowns, plumed hats, gloves and ribbands which were displayed to the dazzled gaze of fashionable ladies of the town and offered for sale at astoundingly low prices. The bargain merchandise rapidly changed hands, but, before the excitement had died away and the packmen were scarcely out of town, the first case of plague had been reported among the unsuspecting population. People were seized with shivering and faintness, buboes developed about their persons and they suffered from bleeding noses. News was passed round that the clothes were contaminated with plague and they were speedily collected and burned, But it was too late. The victims were taken away from the town and buried in a field at Crantock on the north coast.

Also in Cheshire   Chester has its God's Providence House, a picturesque half-timbered house which is said to have derived its name from the fact that it was the only house to escape a visitation of plague.

The disease was possibly carried in personal clothing from London to Bradley in the parish of Malpas, Cheshire, during the July of 1625, and resulted in the death of a complete household. Bearer of the dread disease was Raffe Dawson who had travelled from London 'about 25th July last past, and being sicke of the plague died at his father's house, and soe infected the sayd house and was buryed, as is reported, neare unto his father's howse.'

Then a servant died, followed by a brother and the father, all being 'buried in the night'. Next a sister and a sister-in-law sickened and were buried on the same day. Three days later 'Richarde Dawson being sicke of the plague and perceyving he must die at yt tyme, arose out of his bed, and made his grave and causing his nefew, John Dawson, to cast some strawe into the grave, which was not far from the howse, and went and layd uppon, and soe departed out of this world; this he did, because he was a strong man, and heavier than his said nefew, and another wench were able to burye, he died about the 23rd of August, 1625.'

But neither John nor the 'wench' were able to escape the fate which had befallen kinsmen and employer for 'John Dawson, sonne of the above-named Thomas, came unto his father, when his father sent for him, being sicke, and haveing layd him down in a ditch, died in it the 29th Daye of August, 1625, in the night. Rose Smyth, servant of the above-named Tho: Dawson, and last of yt household, died of the plague, and was buryed by Wm. Cooke, the 5th daye of September, near the sayd house.'

Two of a group of lonely gravestones survive near Bowstones Farm in Cheshire, the others having been applied by some unsentimental farmer for use in his dairy. These stones recall an outbreak at Kettleshulme in 1646 when the unfortunate victims were driven from their homes to this isolated spot. They erected temporary shelters and were supplied with food by more compassionate neighbours or relatives, but gradually grew too weak to collect the provisions from the appointed place. One by one they died and their unburied bodies lay beneath the shelter of a rough stone wall until one man summoned up sufficient courage to dig the shallow graves and give them burial. One of the stones records the death in July, 1646, of Robert Blakewall, while another is quaintly inscribed:

'Think not
Strange ovr
Bones ly here
thine may ly
Thou kno
west not
Where.

Elizabeth
Hampson.'

48

Omens and Predictions Any sensible analysis of causes responsible for the calamity which befel the people of Eyam will give little credence to the stories of a visitation of divine judgment incurred by several wanton youths who had driven a young cow into church while a Wakestime service was in progress. Or because two recusant Catholic priests, arrested at Padley Hall many years before, were alleged to have uttered a curse on Eyam after being verbally abused by its residents when passing through the village. It is also possible that the meteor which had previously been visible was afterwards interpreted by superstitious people as an omen of disaster. An anonymous poet wrote:-

'All friends had met the Wake to celebrate
And dress the wells, but e'er they ceased their mirth
Some spoke of lights in heaven and meteors great,
Some told of wondrous troublings of the earth.'

Perhaps not many people who are familiar with the story of the Great Plague are aware that it was prophesied during a seance held in Cornwall during the year 1665. The story is attested in the diary of the Rev. John Rudall who had been invited to Botathen, a house in the parish of South Petherton, by a certain Mr. Bligh whose son was every day accosted by the ghost of Dorothy Dinglet as he crossed the heath on his way to school. Dressed in a long gown, with one arm held closely to her side and the other stretched out in front of her, her face was white and wearing an anguished expression. She could be clearly seen in broad daylight, and appeared to 'swim' along the ground rather than having a walking motion. It was also observed that she never blinked, even in the strongest sunlight.

Mr. Rudall accompanied the boy and saw the spectre gliding along the grass, whereupon he decided to seek the Bishop of Exeter's approval to conduct a service of exorcism. Consent was reluctantly given.

On January 12th, 1665, Mr. Rudall entered the heath wearing a brass ring on the index finger of his right hand. He paced out and measured a circle on the grass, marking a pentacle in the middle, after which he set up a clutch of rowan and stood facing north. Following further ritual the ghost appeared and was challenged for some sign to prove that it was a 'true spirit and not a false fiend', whereupon Dorothy prophesied that before next Yuletide 'a fearful pestilence would lay waste the land and myriads of souls be loosened from their flesh and the valleys would be full.'

The Plague of London Many accounts of this terrible visitation of London from 1664 to 1666 are in existence. Perhaps one of the most graphic is that contained in the diary of Samuel Pepys—a commentary upon the period which is more fascinating than the chronicles of contemporary historians. Daniel Defoe also wrote a work of fiction entitled *Journal of the Plague Year* which, although it is not recognised as an altogether authentic documentary, nevertheless presents a vivid picture of existing conditions.

Before its appearance in London, the Plague was raging fiercely in Holland and it was suspected that two Frenchmen had introduced the disease in a parcel of woollen goods which came from that country. They lived in Longacre and were seized with the illness after opening the goods. In November, 1663, Pepys recorded a proposal that all vessels from Amsterdam or Hamburg should remain in quarantine for thirty days. On May 4th, 1664, he mentioned that the 'plague increases at Amsterdam', and the following month—when relations between the two countries were somewhat strained—he wrote: 'The talk upon the 'Change is, that De Ruyter is dead, with fifty men of his own ship of the plague, at Calais: that the Holland Ambassador here do endeavour to sweeten us with fair words, and things like to be peaceable.'

In less than a week he made the entry:- 'To the 'change and coffee-house, where great talk of the Dutch preparing of sixty sail of ships. The plague grows mightily among them, both at land and sea.'

The plague had a sobering effect upon the reckless life of the citizens of London. They had not imagined the disease crossing the North Sea and invading their own shores. Gaiety, pride and fashion swayed the city. Many public bodies were dishonest and corrupt. Society was immoral and even the royal house was tainted with shame. Thoughtful people decided that the plague was divinely ordained, recalling the appearance of a comet in 1664 which they considered a warning of impending doom. The comet which gave rise to this misguided theology was mentioned by Pepys:- 'Dec. 17th. Mighty talk there is of this comet that is seen a' nights: and the King and Queen did sit up last night to see it, and did, it seems. And to-night I thought to have done so too: but it is cloudy, and so no stars appear . . . Dec. 24th. I saw the comet, which now, whether worn away or no, I know not, appears not with a tail, but only is larger and duller than any other star . . . Dec. 27th. The comet appeared again to-night, but duskily.'

The following year saw the plague spreading through the city. The Armageddon had begun! London was beseiged by an invisible army as the trampling hooves of the pale horse of pestilence struck down its terrified inhabitants. On the 7th June Pepys wrote:- 'The hottest day that ever I felt in my life. This day, much against my will, I did in Drury Lane see two or three houses marked with a red cross upon the doors, and "Lord, have mercy upon us", writ there; this was a sad sight to me, being the first of this kind that to my remembrance I ever saw.' As we read the accounts written concerning this tragic time, our imagination is haunted by the tolling of bells and the hoarse cries of those who collected the dead. Pest-houses were distinguished by the red crosses and piteous supplications 'Lord, have mercy upon us!' This inscription was the grim slogan of death—a signal of distress which could summon neither rescue nor relief. It was the heraldry of despair.

Sextons could not dig sufficient graves, nor could the carpenters make enough coffins. It was therefore found necessary to close the graveyards and inter the dead in huge pits dug on the outskirts of the city. The silence of night was broken by the ringing of handbells accompanied by the mournful cry, 'Bring out your dead!' Pedestrians recoiled at the sound and shrank furtively into the shadows as the laden carts rumbled along to the sepulchral pits. Here the tumbled bodies were discharged—a naked mass of mortality disfigured by the leprosy of plague and made more revolting by loathsome smells—so horrible a spectacle that even the scavengers of human disease themselves shrank away in dread.

Fire of London The plague virtually ceased with the outbreak of fire in 1665, although isolated cases lingered into the following year. This conflagration, though it multiplied the sorrows of the survivors by destroying their homes, prevented the disease from spreading when all human expedients had failed. Some writers have gone so far as to suggest that it was due to a deliberate act of incendiarism designed to halt the plague. Acres of property were reduced to ruin as the flames hungrily consumed street after street of buildings which were largely made of timber. Many monuments of historical and architectural interest perished in the blaze. Problems created by the plague were now complicated by the fire, and various measures had to be adopted to relieve the hardships of those who, having suffered bereavement, were now rendered homeless and destitute.

The Fire had some compensation apart from having arrested the Plague. The city—cleansed of disease—was now purged of much unhealthy property which had created those conditions favourable to the virus of plague. Thus from the desolation of depopulated areas arose a new and healthier London, and its resurrection was marked by wider streets, better houses, improved sanitation, and a reformation in the architecture of churches and public buildings. But the disease had escaped total extinction for—

> The Plague
> O'er hills and vales of gold and green,
> Passed on undreaded and unseen:
> Foregoing cities, towns and crowds;
> Gay mansions glittering to the clouds,
> Magnificence and wealth,
> To reach a humbler, sweeter spot,
> The village and the peaceful cot,
> The residence of health.   (DR. HOLLAND)

The plague came to Eyam in autumn; that season of the year when the surrounding hills are thatched with purple, when the ripe corn lies in golden sheaves, when the blackberry briars are laden with drooping sprays of fruit, and the trees are dappled with the first tints of yellow, russet and bronze. It came as a stowaway, for the arrival of a consignment of cloth sent from London coincided with an outbreak of the same scourge which had so ruthlessly pruned the population of the capital. And it left the once peaceful village scarred with signs of an awful desolation.

First Victim About the beginning of September, 1665, the tailor in Eyam received a box of textiles from London. Upon examination he found the materials to be damp and innocently put them before the fire to dry. Within a few days he was taken ill and died, after being affected by symptoms which, although perhaps unrecognised at the time, proved beyond doubt the fatal nature of his ailment. Thus the young rector, William Mompesson, made the first solemn entry in the parish register:

'Sept. 7. Buried George Viccars,'

little aware that this was but the initial name in a long list of obituaries.

Rev. William Mompesson

Mompesson's Well
Courtesy of "The Stamp Magazine"

Plague Cottages (after Sir Francis Chantrey)
Courtesy of "The Stamp Magazine"

In a medical work entitled *A Discourse of the Plague*, published in 1720, Dr. Richard Mead gives a description of the singular circumstances by which the disease reached Eyam. 'The plague was likewise at Eyam, in the Peak of Derbyshire; being brought thither by means of a box sent from London to a taylor in that village, containing some materials relating to his trade. A servant who opened the aforesaid box, complaining that the goods were damp, was ordered to dry them by the fire; but in so doing it was seized with the plague and died; the same misfortune extended itself to the rest of the family, except the taylor's wife who alone survived. From hence the distemper spread about, and destroyed in that village, and the rest of the parish, though a small one, between two and three hundred persons. But notwithstanding this so great violence of the disease, it was restrained from reaching beyond that parish by the care of the Rector; from whose son, and another worthy gentleman, I have the relation. The clergyman advised that the sick should be removed into huts or barracks, built upon the common; and procuring, by the interest of the then Earl of Devonshire, that the people should be well furnished with provisions, he took effectual care that no one should go out of the parish, and by this means he protected his neighbourhood with complete success.'

Although it may seem presumptuous to question the authority of George Mompesson, who jointly supplied the doctor with his information, yet the facts of history do not altogether agree with his testimony. According to long established tradition (borne out by the parish register), it was not a servant, but the tailor himself who opened the box, arrayed the materials before the fire and was seized with the plague. Nor, as far as is known, was the tailor married, the person referred to being Widow Cooper with whom Viccars lodged. This confusion of facts, after so short a time, helps to show how unreliable can be the evidence supplied by memory and oral testimony.

Plague Cottage   The cottage in which the plague claimed its first victim is situated a few paces west of the Church. At that time it was the joint property of Jonathan and Edward, sons of the late Edward Cooper, a lead-miner who had purchased the house in 1662 and who died two years later. Under the conditions of his will, provision was made whereby the widow should have a life interest in the property, but Providence decreed that she should survive both her sons who were early victims of the plague. She afterwards married a certain John Coe. It is therefore concluded that George Viccars was a journeyman tailor lodging at the time with the Cooper family.

Discovery of the Disease   No doubt there were discreet attempts to conceal the cause of Viccar's death, but when Edward Cooper died a fortnight later having shown similar symptoms, it would not be so easy to suppress whispered suspicions as to the character of the disease, and when Peter Halksworth, a neighbour, died the next day and Thomas Thorpe after three more days, then pretence and secrecy must have been in vain. Especially when two further deaths occurred on the last day of September, followed by two each on the 1st and 3rd of October. As the tumours tightened their stranglehold on the throat of each victim, and the plague spot continued to blossom on their chests like the deadly nightshade of death, the villagers were horrified to realise the danger to which they had been so suddenly and unexpectedly exposed. Yet this was but the shadow of the destroying angel's wing!

Six solemn processions to the churchyard had been seen during September.

Among certain documents which have recently come to light, the will of William Thorpe shows how promptly some of the villagers reacted to the emergency by making preparation for the disposal of their property in the event of their being overtaken by the disaster. His son, Thomas, appears to have been the fourth victim, perhaps due to his involvement in giving neighbourly assistance when Viccars was taken ill. The sixth victim, Mary Thorpe who died on the 30th September, may have been his wife for she is not mentioned in the will. Elizabeth (died 1st October), Mary (died 3rd October) and William (died 7th October) were probably his children or grandchildren, or one of the females may have been the widow of Thomas. William's foresight was not in vain, for he died on the 7th October, and was followed by beneficiaries named in his will—Thomas (died 19th October), Alice (died 15th April, 1666), Robert and William (died May 2nd, 1666) and Thomas and Robert (died 22nd July, 1666). One of the two Roberts was William's eldest grandchild. An Elizabeth Thorpe died on the 8th July, 1666, and a Richard on the 6th August, 1666, although they may have belonged to a different family.

In the name of God Amen. I William Thorpe of Eyam in the County of Darby yeoman beinge in good health and perfect memory blessed be god, but seeing by dayly experience the uncertainty of this transitory life by the hand of god upon my family Do make constitute ordaine and declare this my last will and Testament in manner and forme following. Revokinge and anullinge (by these presents) all and every Testament and Testaments, will and wills heretofore by me made and declared, eyther by word or writinge, and this to be taken onely for my last will and Testament and none other.

I committe my soule unto Almighty God, being fully assured, through his mercy, by the merits of Jesus Christ my Saviour and Redeemer to be saved eternally: and my body to the earth, to be buried at the discretion of my Executor hereafter named. And concerning my worldly estate my will and minde is as followeth.

All my goods and Chattels, moveable and unmoveable whatsoever, I give and bequeath (my debts and funerall first payed and discharged) unto Thomas Thorpe and Alice Thorpe, or the survivor of them, being son and daughter of my son Thomas Thorpe late deceased, for and towards theire bringinge up and education.

I give and bequeath unto Alice Thorpe my grandechilde aforesayd, fifteene pounds, to be payed out of my lands, when she shall accomplish the age of one and twenty years.

All my housinge and lands, I give and bequeath unto William Thorpe and Thomas Thorpe aforesayd or the survivor of them and to their heyrs, lawfully to be begotten. And for want of such issue my will and minde is That my said lands and housings returns to Robert Thorpe, eldest son of my sayd son Thomas Thorpe and to the heyrs of his Body lawfully to be begotten. And for want of such issue to Alice Thorpe aforesayd and to her heyrs lawfully to be begotten. And for want of such issue, my will and minde is, and I doe hereby declare it to be my Reall will and minde, that the said lands and housing goe, remaine, and be to and for the only use and behoofe of Abraham Broadhurst my wellbeloved cousin, son of George Broadhurst of Upper Haddon, and to his heyrs and assigns for ever.

Lastly I give and bequeath unto Robert Thorpe and William Thorpe aforesayd, eyther of them twenty shillings to be payd in one whole yeare after my descease. And I doe nominate and appoint John Wilson of Church-Style and the sayd Abraham

Broadhurst Guardians to the sayd Alice Thorpe and Thomas Thorpe: and Executir of this my last will and Testament desiring them to take this charge upon them not doubting but they will execute it accordinge to the true intent and meanings thereof. In witness whereof I have hereunto putt my hand and seale The third day of October 1665.

In the presence of us   William Thorpe
John Hancock
John Chapman his marke
Anthony Raworth

The month of October showed an alarming increase in the death rate for twenty-three people died. The virulence of the plague was, however, arrested by the approach of winter, for only seven deaths were registered in November and it was fervently hoped that the frost and snow would destroy this pestilence which was known to flourish best in the hot and humid conditions of sub-tropical climates. But this optimism was ill-founded in spite of the welcome diminution in the number of deaths. The winter is said to have been severe, and those familiar with the moods of the Peak District at this season of the year can well imagine the village lying silent and shrouded with snow. The cottage eaves would be fringed with icicles hanging like naked daggers, and every crevice in the walls would be plastered with driven snow. Deep drifts would make the narrow lanes inaccessible, completely sealing off the village from the outside world.

Nine victims succumbed during December, five in January, and eight in February.

Graves at Bretton   Less than two miles from Eyam, the hamlet of Bretton is perched conspicuously upon the spine of Hucklow Edge. During February the seeds of pestilence were sown in this isolated spot, maturing in a harvest of five victims. Bretton—bleak and lonely in situation—consists of a few farmsteads near the old Barrel Inn. Close to one of the farmhouses, which has now been converted into a youth hostel, five sunken stones perpetuate the sad event. Upon one of these we discern the initials of Peter Mortin (although the M looks more like an H) who died on the 4th February, 1666.

Victim at Foolow   A flying spark from the fire which was smouldering in Eyam also alighted among the residents of Foolow. Fortunately it appears to have been extinguished with the death and burial, during March, of a certain Mary Buxton; yet some family living in this remote spot became fellow mourners with the citizens of far-off London! Foolow is a hamlet lying two miles west of Eyam. Its cottages are built of grey limestone and nestle within the shadow of a few trees which afford some protection from the gales that sweep over the bleak country-side.

Down in the woods, among the ivied crags of limestone, the snowdrops had risen from their dark sepulchres of soil. Crocuses were intruding in cottage gardens, as though attempting to relieve the famine of colour caused by the locust appetite of winter. The cold, corpse-like earth was responding to the gentle respiration of spring, and soon this welcome season produced its inevitable resurrection to life. The winged orchestra of nature began to gladden the woods with its ministry of song; flowers, which had slept long and silently in the dark womb of the earth, now burst open the sheaths embalming their dewy petals, and butterflies with silken wings began to flit to and fro in the sunlight. Bleating lambs frisked in fields starred with daisies and celandines. Naked trees became clothed with garments of transparent green as the timid buds discarded their swaddling bands. Primroses and violets appeared about the roots of twisted thorn-trees, as the earth was refreshed and revitalized with sunshine and shower. Cattle grazed contentedly in the meadows, and the sower was to be seen striding along brown furrows corrugated by the plough as he scattered his seed, sowing—sowing in anticipation that he would reap the golden harvest in autumn.

But, while Nature was everywhere awakening her family from sleep, death was relentlessly claiming the village for its habitation.

Rowland and Emmot   The story of Emmot Sydall and Rowland Torre—son of a Stoney Middleton flour-miller—is a story of thwarted romance, yet a story which has captured the sympathy and imagination of many people. Emmot lived in a thatched cottage near the Church. Living opposite to the cottage where the lightning of plague had struck its first victim, we find that the Sydall family had early contracted the infection. Emmot's father, brother and four sisters died during the second month of the Plague. During those days of overwhelming sorrow, Rowland sought to comfort and console his sweetheart with many soothing and tender ministries. This was the therapy she needed to heal the wounds inflicted by her grief. Yet she tearfully urged him not to expose himself to peril by continuing his visits, but he passionately insisted. At length he relented to her persuasions and they agreed to meet in the Delph not far from Emmot's home.

At the end of April, Emmot's name was added to the list of dead.

Imagination cannot enter into the anguish of the mother—sole survivor of the family. Almost demented by grief, and utterly unable to endure the loneliness of her ravished home, she fled to relatives who had found refuge in huts built in the Delph.

Meanwhile, Rowland's visits to the accustomed trysting-place were unrewarded by any glimpse of the girl he loved and whom he had planned to marry the following Wakes. Rumours of her death filtered through to him and the sorrowful tidings were confirmed by her continued absence. When the plague ceased Rowland was among the first who ventured to enter the village. Before reaching the cottage where he had enjoyed many happy experiences—experiences existing now only as memories tinged with unutterable woe—he encountered one of the survivors, an urchin in the street, and he tactfulessly blurted out: 'Ah! Rowland, thy Emmot's dead and buried in Cussy Dell.'

Danger of Panic   The population had already begun to shrink by evacuation as well as by death. Wealthy inhabitants vacated their homes with haste and sought refuge elsewhere. Bradshaw Hall was deserted by the widow of Squire George Bradshaw and her daughter, Ann. An influential family named Sheldon took up their abode at a house they owned at Hazleford. Some ducks they had taken with them were apparently discontented with their new surroundings, and, guided by instinct waddled across the moors back to Eyam. Another family built a hut near Riley. Andrew Merril and his cockerel lived in a shack near the summit of Sir William Hill. One day Merril was deserted by his feathered friend which showed some agitation, crowed noisily, and then took to its wings and flew away in the direction of Eyam. Arguing to himself that the instincts of the bird were probably superior to his own, Andrew decided to risk returning home and found that the plague had spent its fury. He also found the bird re-established in its old environment.

Recognising that a general panic might develop as a result of this exodus, the Rector urged his parishioners to stay, pointing out the dangers of scattering the seeds of infection by unrestrained flight. Inspired more by Mompesson's example than by his eloquence, they accepted what amounted to virtual immolation that the disease might be confined within the parish. Thus the steady drainage of people who were thoughtlessly exposing others to peril was checked and the residue covenanted with their Rector so that the security of those outside the village might be assured. Nor was it an easy decision to make, for villages in those days—more so even than today—were closely-knit communities of relatives and friends. When sorrow crossed the threshold of one family, it entered the hearts and homes of the entire village to be shared by all. Therefore, as the tide of death crept slowly forward, each funeral was that of a relative, a friend or a neighbour.

Flakes of the snowy blossom of hawthorn trees which abound along the hillside and in the dales, fluttered like confetti to the ground as spring melted into summer. Some writer has said that 'there is a tradition that the smell of the Great Plague of London remains in the flowers . . . May blossom and plague were part of one another, associated with death.' Perhaps this same tradition had credence in Eyam, for it is still considered unlucky to take May blossom into houses and is claimed to be an augury of death.

Plague Boundaries Although the village would be to some extent self-supporting in fruit, vegetables, meat and perhaps in producing flour, the procuring of certain foods, medicines and other supplies threatened to be a serious problem until the co-operation of the Earl of Devonshire was enlisted by Mompesson who had early acquainted him of the situation created by the people's voluntary isolation. The Earl arranged for provisions, clothing and medical supplies to be left at certain points on a boundary which had been specified by Mompesson. These points were ususaly identified by stone troughs in which money paid for the goods could be deposited. Vinegar was poured into the water in the belief that its mild acid action would ensure disinfection of the coins. A record was also kept of the mounting mortality and this was left, together with a list of requirements, at the places selected.

Mompesson's Well Situated between Eyam and Hathersage, Mompesson's Well consists of a trough hewn out of stone which has been dignified by the addition of a canopy of stone moulded into a diagonal cross. Another site between Eyam and Stoney Middleton is marked by a boulder in the top of which several holes have been bored. Food was brought to both these places by persons responsible for provisioning the isolated village. Bread was brought from Hazleford by a man named Cooper and was left upon a certain boulder near the Wet Withins circle. Another person is said to have brought victuals from Little

Common, then a hamlet near Sheffield. Brick ovens were pointed out at Bubnell where bread was said to have been baked and brought to the bottom of Eyam Dale, money being washed in the brook.

Plague stones are to be found in many parts of the country, although their authenticity cannot always be as readily substantiated as those at Eyam. In some places they are known as 'leper stones' or 'penny stones' and it is not unlikely that Pennistone, near Sheffield, derived its name from the former existence of such a stone. The city of York has several stones which tradition claims to have had association with plagues. These include the Fulford Stone, said to have been used for washing coins in 1665 and again in 1823 during an epidemic of cholera. It also has the Burton Stone; a cross plinth thought to have been adapted for the same purpose in 1603-4 by the cutting of four additional basins in the surface. Many such stones up and down the country were no doubt improvised in times of plague for this purpose; whereas others have been given such ascriptions by the vagaries of rustic imagination which has more respect for tradition than for truth, and has often been guilty of transmuting 'fact' into fiction for the sake of sheer sensationalism.

Ex-Rector Co-operates   The emergency created by this common peril united the Rector and one of his predecessors, the Rev. Thomas Stanley. By their combined efforts they restored some measure of composure among the panic-stricken people to whom they had been called as ministers. Stanley had been dispossessed of the Eyam living when outlawed from the Established Church because of his sympathies with Parliament and because of the demands made by the Corporation Act, Five Mile Act and Act of Uniformity. Reconciled—if they were ever otherwise—in the hour of danger by their mutual obligations, both Conformist and Nonconformist counselled their followers to remain within the boundary to stay the spread of infection. Persuaded of the terrible risks involved by flight, the people accepted the onus of this covenant which, almost without exception, appears to have been faithfully observed.

There are only two instances on record of people deserting the village.

The Woman from Orchard Bank   One woman fugitive ventured to Tideswell where the authorities had taken strict measures to prevent infection reaching their town. They had posted a guard whose business it was to interrogate any strangers approaching from the direction of Eyam, and to refuse admission to any suspected residents of that village. When confronted by the sentry, the woman evaded his questions in the following war of wits:

'Woman, whence comest thou?'
'From Orchard Bank',
'And where is that?'
'Why, verily, 'tis in the land of the living!' was her naive retort.

The sentry, whose knowledge of geography was evidently too vague to discover her deception, allowed the woman to pass without further question. Having taken the precaution to project her scheme on market day, she furtively mingled with the crowd, but was recognised almost immediately. Swiftly the warning cry ran through the busy throng:

58

'The plague! the plague! a woman from Eyam!'

Realising that her scheme was thwarted, the discomfited woman fled from the town with an angry mob in pursuit. A shower of stones, clods of turf, and other missiles encouraged her retreat. Dejectedly she returned to her home, 'a sadder but wiser woman' as the result of her unsuccessful escapade.

Other townships had taken similar precautions to intercept possible refugees. The Sheffield Constables had a record in their accounts concerning 'Charges about keeping people from Fulwood Spring at the time the plague was at Eyam.' The restrictions imposed upon the stranger by various public authorities were so stringent that even fuel had to be obtained by falsehood. Carters, entrusted with the difficult mission of securing supplies of coal, are said to have adopted various expedients in achieving their object and often had recourse to the art of mendacity after having taken circuitous routes to reach the collieries. Having disguised his identity by false statements, one fellow unguardedly referred to the epidemic raging in his village and was driven away with a tumult of threats and imprecations.

White Watson tells of the precautions taken at Bakewell to prevent unwelcome visitors from Eyam. He wrote:- 'The brook near Stockingcote is called Monday Brook because when the Plague was in Eyam in 1666 they used to come to market and to put their money into this rivulet, and were not permitted to come near either town. The market day was on Monday.'

The Bubnell Carter Reasons for flight are quite obvious, but those of a person who entered the village in defiance of persuasion and entreaty, are difficult to understand. Yet one fellow—a carter from Bubnell who worked on the Chatsworth estate—was instructed to convey a load of timber either to Eyam, or somewhere in the vicinity. His neighbours, recognising the hazards of such a journey, used every argument to dissuade him from the venture; but still he persisted in going. Upon the appointed day the carter arrived at his destination, but was unable to find anyone to assist in unloading the wagon. Nor did he find the task of unloading single-handed improved by a steady drizzle which fell while he was doing the work. Upon returning home in his wet clothes he developed the symptoms of a chill; symptoms which were not unnaturally mistaken by his neighbours as evidence of infection by plague.

Rumours that the carter had fallen victim to the plague spread rapidly through the district and a neighbour was forthwith appointed as a vigilante to watch his cottage and raise the alarm if he should attempt to leave. Some even threatened to shoot him if he so much as crossed his threshold! The predicament of the carter, whose arrogance had now evaporated and who was regretting his own folly, was brought to the notice of the Earl of Devonshire and he made arrangements that his personal physician should examine the man to diagnose his complaint. Taking no risks, the patient was instructed to stand on the Bubnell side of the River Derwent while the doctor questioned him from the opposite bank. The carter on one side of the river—the doctor on the other! Such were the unique circumstances under which the examination was conducted, but it was ultimately decided that the suspected disease was nothing more than a severe cold and the carter was released (no doubt reluctantly) from quarantine. The prescription given by the doctor to the carter was preserved at Barlow, but now appears to be lost.

Incidentally, I have read somewhere that the Cavendish family did not escape the sorrows of the Plague, for one its sons, who was a pupil of Thomas Hobbes, the philosopher, died of the disease.

In view of the threatened extermination of Eyam people, a young woman who had recently married a resident of Curbar, secretly visited the stricken village to see her widowed mother. She found her dying of the plague. Returning hurriedly to Curbar, she herself developed the fatal symptoms and expired in agony after the lapse of two days. To the great relief of her neighbours the disease did not spread. Thirty years before, the same dread pestilence had visited their homes and the recollection of that brief but awful occasion was still a vivid memory.

Cucklet Church In an effort to safeguard the health of those who had hitherto succeeded in evading infection, the Rector decided to close the Church for worship in order to segregate members of his congregation from each other. Thus, about the month of June,

> Contagion closed the portals of the fane:
> He then a temple sought, not made with hands,
> But reared by Him, amidst whose works it stood,
> Rudely magnificent.
>
> (ROBERTS)

In the Delph a solitary crag of limestone is honeycombed with a series of caverns. From a distance it rather resembles a huge skull lying on the hillside, and could well merit the Hebrew name, Golgotha (Place of a Skull). This was the site chosen by Mompesson as an alternative meeting-place for worship, and in the shadow of this grotto church, with its vaulted masonry eaten away by centuries of erosion, the Rector and his ever diminishing congregation met twice each Sunday and sometimes during the week for their devotions. Here they found a brief respite from the horrors of physical disease and death; and here they found healing for the wounds and afflictions of the spirit. And it is here at this place—hallowed by such solemn associations that it has become renowned as Cucklet Church—that we feel a strange affinity with the stricken people as they marked the incessant shrinkage in attendance. Orphans, widows, and childless parents—a broken-hearted people—stood silently apart in this valley of shadow. It was the Gethsemane of their experience as they echoed the prayer for deliverance: 'Father, if Thou be willing, let this cup pass—nevertheless not my will . . . '

Nineteen deaths were recorded in June, but the following month witnessed scenes of inexpressible grief with the death of fifty-six people.

Riley House Tomb The music of the anvil ceased at Riley! No longer the glowing coals leaped into flame in response to the panting bellows, no gush of sparks showered from the white-hot iron on the anvil, no hollow clink of metal echoed to the usual ringing blows of the smith. Imagination peeps into the silent smithy with its extinguished fire, and sees the heavy sledge reared against the anvil. Pincers, hammers and nail-boxes lie among the assortment of rusty shoes, broken chains and implements. There is no acrid smell of scorching hot iron being plunged into cold water. An uncanny stillness prevails. Richard

Talbot had combined the occupation of smith with that of farmer, but during July both he and his wife and their family of five died of the disease. One son, who was absent from home at the time, was the only survivor. Before he had died, Talbot had dictated his will to the Rector who, in a moment of mental aberration had written his own name during the introductory paragraph and then scored it out with a series of loops made by the pen before inserting that of the smith. It may also be that the Rector was under such pressure that he could not remember the date for the actual day of month is left a blank.

'In ye name of God Amen, I Richard Talbot of Ryley in ye County of Derby Yeoman, being sick and weak but in good memory, do make this my last will and testament in manner and forme following. First I bequeath my soul into ye hands of God who made me, depending my salvation upon the account of Jesus Christ my Redeemer, my body to be buried at the discretion of my Executor. My estate I dispose as followeth.

'First I give all my estate to my loving wife Catherine Talbot (if she marry not again) but if she should marry again a third part of my estate only, out of which fair estate she is to give my eldest son Robert Talbott a heifer called Buxton heifer: and the smithy shop to George Talbott my son paying upon the day of his marriage five pounds to the said Robert Talbott. If the said George dye then the smithy shop to go to Jonathan my third son, if all my children dye then I give my whole estate to be divided equally between Jonathan Hunstone of Ashton under Lyne in ye County of Lancashire and Joseph Bramhall of Ryley aforesaid to be equally divided between them and if the said Joseph dye then his moyety to be distributed among the poor of Eyam parish according to the discretion of my executor and lastly I make William Mompesson Rector of Eyam Executor of this my last will and Testament witness my hand and this   of July 1666.

<table>
<tr><td>Sealed & signed
in ye presence of
    his
Rob: R. Fydler
    marke
    his
Fran: F. Blackwell
    marke</td><td>   his
Rich: T. Talbott
     marke</td></tr>
</table>

Talbot's three daughters, Bridget and Mary (both died on the 5th July) and Ann (who had died two days later) are not mentioned in the will and were obviously dead before it was made. A Jane Talbot died on the 17th July, the day before the mother, but she appears to have been a member of another family for a Joan and Ruth died on the 26th., the day following the father's death. The two brothers who figured in the will, but who never benefited from its terms, were Robert who died the day before his father and Jonathan whose death occurred on the 30th of the month. George was the survivor and is mentioned on the Hearth Tax roll of 1670.

Talbot was evidently a man of substance for the inventory of his goods amounted to £126 7s, and this document makes interesting, if pathetic, reading, for there is reference to three stools and spinning-wheels which must have been the property of the daughters. One item—a silver spoon—was valued at five shillings.

In the orchard of the present Riley House, a tombstone perpetuates this tragedy of family life.

The cooper's bench, with its tools scattered among crisp wood shavings, was now sprinkled with dust, pathetically indicating the death of Rowland Mower who made casks and barrels for the lead-mines and other trades. This craftsman's will is also extant. The document was probably compiled by Joseph Stanley, a Chesterfield attorney and brother to the nonconforming Thomas who was a signatory to the will.

'In the Name of God Amen. The sixe & twentieth day of June Ano dnj 1666 I Rowland Mower of Eyam in the county of Derby, Cooper, beinge of good & pfect memory and Vnderstandinge. (blessed be God for it) but consideringe God Almightys heavy visitation vpon this Towne of Eyam, & vpon my owne Family at this psent: Doe make & ordaine this my last will and Testamt in manner & forme following: vizt First and principally I doe bequeath & resigne vp my soule into the hands of Almight God: Hopeing through the merits of Jesus Christ my Saviour & Redeemer to inherit eternal life: And my body to the earth: when it shall please the Lord to call me hence: to be interred accordinge to the discretion of my friends: And as for such Worldly Estate as well Real as Psonall as it hath pleased the Lord to endowe me withall, I doe give, bequeath & dispose thereof as followeth, vizt Impr. I doe give & bequeath vnto John Torre of Eyam aforesaid my brother in Law the sume of tenne shillings of Lawful English money: Item. I doe give & bequeath vnto Robt. Masland my naturall brother tweluepence: Item. I doe give & bequeath vnto Elizabeth the wife of Henry Clarke my naturall Sister the sume of tenne shillings of like lawful English money: Ite. I doe give, bequeath, & leave the sum of fforty shillings of like lawful English money, to be putt forth shortly after my decease, into safe hands for the use & behalfe of the poore of the towne of Eyam: And the yearly Interest and Pfit thereof to be distributed at the Feast of the Nativity of our Lord yearly to the most necessitous poore of Eyam towne accordinge to the discretion of the Minister & Overseer of the poore of Eyam aforesayd for ever. Ite. I doe give a bequeath vnto Thomas Bockinge, Robert Bockinge & Edyth Bockinge the children of Francis Bockinge of Eyam aforesayd each of them ffive shillings. Ite. I doe give & bequeath vnto each of the children of James Mower, Thomas Ragge, & William Abell of Eyam aforesaid twelue pence a piece. Ite. I doe give & bequeath vnto Thomas Stanley of Eyam aforesayd Clerke the sume of fforty shillings of like lawful English money: Ite. My will and minde is & I doe by these pesents devise, order, & appoynt That Jane French my Tenant shall have & enjoy the house wherein she now dwelleth, payinge to my heyrs & Assignes at the Feast of Pentecost the yearly rent of twopence (if it be lawfully demanded) for & during the time of her naturall life. The rest of my worldly goods and chattels whatsoever moueable and vnmoueable, quicke and dead, together with all my houses lands & Real Estate (my debts Legacies & funeral expenses first payed and discharged). I doe give, bequeath, & leave vnto Elizabeth my beloved wife, & Rowland my naturall son, & to the longer liuer of them two: That is to say: If 't Please the Lord to take away my sayd son Rowland, & my wife to live: Then my will and minde is that she shall haue & enjoy not only my goods and chattels but alsoe all my houses & lands for and duringe the terme of her naturall Life: And if she be now with childe then I doe leave & appoynt the sayd childe, be it son or daughter, to be my lawfull heyre to all my Real estate: And if she bringe forth a man-childe & both it & my son Rowland doe live: Then I doe leave and appoynt them to be co-heyrs to all my houses & lands And my sayd wife to have the moity or one halfe thereof duringe her life as aforesayd: And my sayd son or sons to enter vpon & have the other moity or halfe thereof, when he or they shall accomplish his or their age or ages of one & twenty years: But if my sayd wife depart this life and leave behind her any Issue by me, vnder the age of one & twenty years: Then I do hereby nominate and appoynt Henry Clarke my brother in Law, & Elizabeth his wife my naturall Sister, Guardians over & for such my Issue to manage my Estate for their Education, till they come to age. But if it shall please the Lord to take away both my sayd son Rowland, & my sayd wife without any of my Issue left behinde her: Then my will & minde is, & I do hereby give, bequeath & dispose of all my wordly Estate both Reall & Psonall (besides the Legacies afore bequeathed) as followeth. That is to say. Impr. I doe give & bequeath the sume of six pounds, over & besides the afore bequeathed sume of fforty shillings (that is to say, eight pounds in the whole) to be putt forth shortly after the longer liver of my sayd wife and son by my heyrs Executes & Assignes to be employed, improved, & distributed to & for the poore of the towne of Eyam, according as is before herein mentioned & expressed for ever. Ite. I do give & bequeath vnto George Cooper my true and lawfull Apprentice the sume of Four pounds beinge the sume which his father Abraham Cooper gave me with him to be returned to him together with his indentures for his best Advantage frome & after the decease of my sayd wife & son. Ite. I doe give & bequeath vnto Hannah Cocker my Niece the Tenant-right of my house with the Apptnces in Froggatt. Ite. I doe give & bequeath vnto John Torre my brother in Law aforesayd all my cowper-wares wood & tools whatsoever: And alsoe all that my Close or pcel of land enclosed, comonly called & knowne by the name of Shininge-cliffe in Eyam aforesayd, for & duringe only the terme of the naturall life of him the sayd John Torre: And the rest of all my wordly Estate as well Reall as Psonall together with the Revertion, Inheritance & Remainder of the sayd close called Shining-cliffe I doe give bequeath & leave vnto my naturall Sister Elizabeth Clarke aforenamed, for and during the terme of her naturall life: And afterwards vnto Jonathan Cocker, George & John Clarke her three sons equally amongst them, and their heyrs for ever. And lastly I doe nominate & appoynt Elizabeth my sayd wife & Henry Clarke my brother in Law, Joyntly & Severally Executes of this my last will & Testam. to Pforme all things herein mentioned to my intente: And I do hereby revoke & make void all former wills: And this only to be my last Will & Testam. In witness I have putt my hand and Seale ye day & year first above written.

ROWLAND MOWER
his X marke.

Sealed, signed & delivered in the presence of us

Tho: Stanley
Jo: Stanley,
William Ainsworth.'

Rowland died on the 29th July and his son, Rowland, the day after, but the wife and mother, Elizabeth, survived. Six of the intended beneficiaries from the will also died.

Plague Sexton The usual offices performed immediately after death had long since been discontinued. There was no time for either sentiment or ceremony. Bodies were either dragged by a towel, or carried on an improvised bier, to the waiting grave. Nor were the burials attended by any religious ritual: no solemn recital from the prayer-book—no sprinkling of earth. No flowers and herbs were scattered before the funeral processions of unmarried girls as of yore. Nor were any funeral garlands carried before the cortege to be afterwards hung from the church rafters as mementoes of their chastity. The pathetic rites and ceremonies which usually marked such occasions had been abandoned by common consent. Those incapable of burying their dead relatives assigned the unpleasant task to Marshall Howe; a man whose temerity in discharging the self-appointed duties of sexton created a sense of profound awe and astonishment among the survivors. Possessing a powerful physique and other qualities essential for this undesirable

Well Dressing 1965. "News of the Plague" *Courtesy of "The Buxton Advertiser"*

Well Dressing 1961. Eyam Windmill (after John Platts)

work, he claimed exemption from the plague because he had recovered from a slight infection of the disease and believed himself immune from further attack. This principle of vaccination seems to have been generally accepted at the time. Howe compensated himself for his ghoulish work by rifling the homes of those he had buried with so little of reverence or respect. At the village ale-house in post-plague days, he would boastingly entertain the company with an inventory of his illicit plunder, adding that he had 'pinners and napkins enough to kindle his pipe while he lived.'

Recovery of Victims Marshall Howe's recovery was not an exception, although only a few who received the death sentence of plague were acquitted. One girl —Margaret Blackwell—was seriously ill and in a delirious condition. Seizing a vessel containing scalding bacon fat, she drank the contents in an attempt to satiate her maddening thirst. Her brother, who had cooked the bacon for his breakfast before making a journey to obtain coal, scarcely expected to find Margaret still alive upon his return home. He was astounded therefore to find her considerably better by evening, and this improvement continued until she eventually recovered. Ever afterwards she attributed her recovery to this unusual and unprescribed prophylactic!

The pathetic paragraphs of plague history are occasionally punctuated with incidents which appeal to our sense of humour. Marshall Howe had heard of the expected death of a man named Unwin whose home was at the Town Head, so, without making further enquiry, he quickly prepared a grave in the fellow's orchard. Having completed these preparations, he entered the bedroom and hauled the still warm body of Unwin upon his broad back. Just as he was in the act of descending the stairs, he was startled by the faint voice of the 'corpse' requesting a posset—a mixture of boiled milk, ale, bread and other ingredients. Disgusted at this unexpected turn of events, Howe lowered his scarcely conscious burden to the treads of the stairs and left the house without making any attempt to relieve the poor fellow's distress. Eventually Unwin recovered sufficiently to obtain his posset and survived the ordeal.

We may well compare the villagers with the Roman soldiers garrisoned at Pompeii. When the city was overwhelmed with waves of volcanic lava, they remained rigidly at their post to be buried in the molten stream and embalmed within a tomb of granite. Providence, however, concealed the future peril from the vision of the stricken community of Eyam. Eyes that were almost drained of tears were to weep still more copiously, and hearts, already bleeding with anguish, were to be broken again and yet again.

During August the scourge raged even more fiercely. The majority of families were now dismembered, some being completely annihilated. With unrelaxing vigilance the two ministers pursued their work of visiting the sick, soothing them by the application of whatever antidotes were available. Yet, in spite of all their exertions, the plague persisted. No doubt the villagers had long since exhausted the resources of their own dispensary—remedies distilled from the herbs which grew in abundance upon the heath and in the meadows. Temporary shacks and huts had been built near Riley, along the Edgeside and beneath the rocks in Farnsley Lane and the Delph, but these were relentlessly emptied of their occupants.

Graves at Shepherd's Flatt The poignancy of one incident is without parallel. A family named Mortin lived at the farm known as Shepherd's Flatt midway between Eyam and Foolow, and nearby lived a widow named Mrs. Kempe, whose children—having been in contact with infected playmates at Eyam—were responsible for bringing the plague to the two lonely houses. A baby was expected in the former family, and sometime during August the period of Mrs. Mortin's pregnancy expired. Her husband's frantic appeals for the services of a midwife were bluntly refused. Moreover, the situation was complicated by the eldest child, who, having the disease and being confined to a room, was screaming almost continuously. There was no other alternative but for the harrassed husband to perform the office of midwife, and under these painful circumstances the miracle of incarnation was made complete. Shortly afterwards the mother and her three children died and were buried close to their home. Mortin himself survived and lived for some time in solitude, except for the companionship of Flash, his favourite greyhound.

Stones erected as memorials of this sad event, and which marked the exact place of burial, are said to have been destroyed about 150 years afterwards. Details of later investigation by a descendant of the Mortin family, somewhat contradict the above statement and were supplied to the writer as follows:- 'The names of the children buried by Matthew at the gable end of the house were Robert aged three, Sarah aged two, and a few days' old babe, a son. On the plague tally at the end of the shippen, once the old house, Matthew has carved the initials of the older children and then added a small letter "s", for the little son who died unbaptised.'

This sad story had a sequel, however, which gave it a sunset ending. Some while after the plague had ended, the greyhound suddenly deserted its master who was sitting outside the back door, to form a first-sight friendship with a woman walking along the hillside. Mortin reasoned in his own mind that the faithful animal had mistaken the figure for that of its former mistress. The incident resulted in the formation of a friendship which ended at the altar, for the woman was Sarah Halksworth who had been widowed at the beginning of the Plague. She is thought to have lived next to the Plague Cottage and that her husband, Peter, was the third victim.

This story shows how the fragrant flowers of womanhood and sweet buds of promise—children—were alike blasted by the whirlwind of death. Within a few months the village had been reduced from a collection of homes sheltering happy and healthy families to one vast charnel-house; for every remaining resident was a mourner and almost every residence a mortuary.

Riley Graves Many people are acquainted with the sad history of Riley Graves—an enclosure on the hillside about half a mile from the village. During the calamitous month of August, the farm near that of the Talbots was visited by the plague. Only three days after the extinction of the Talbot family, both John and Elizabeth Hancock died and were buried a short distance from their home. Four days later, the father and his two sons—William and Oner—were each stricken and buried on the seventh day of the month. Two days elapsed and the body of Alice was laid to rest in the private cemetery and upon the following day the sorrowing mother excavated a grave for her remaining daughter, Ann.

Who can imagine the anguish and despair of this woman as she shovelled the earth into that sepulchre containing the last fruits of affectionate parenthood? Unable to endure the loneliness of her plague-ravished home, she fled from the district to spend her remaining days with a son apprenticed to the cutlery trade in Sheffield. It was one of his descendants who erected the stones which identified the place of burial: originally these were laid flat on the ground, but were collected together and surrounded by a stone fence at the instigation of an Eyam antiquary.

In his *Call of England*, H. V. Morton wrote of Riley Graves: 'I think the most touching Plague relic in Eyam is a little cluster of graves in a field some distance from the village. They are protected from wandering cattle by a low stone wall. They are very lonely, with the wind blowing over them, the green moss eating into them, and about them still an air of haste and disaster.'

Bridget's Bible   During August another member of the Talbot family died. This was Bridget Talbot who was probably sister-in-law to the farmer-blacksmith, for one of his daughters had been called Bridget. The elder Bridget's name has recently assumed interest by the discovery of her 'memorandum', or informal will, which is a further specimen of the caligraphy of William Mompesson whose four years' old son, George, had a rather pathetic interest in the contents. The undated document reflects the urgency of the peak month of the Plague:

"Memorandum yt Briget Talbott of Eyam in ye County of Darby: Did give & bequeath all her estate to George Talbott of Eyam aforesaid excepting a Bible to George Mompefson son to Wm. Mompefson of Eyam Church; in ye hearing of

Mary M. Darby.'

Death of Mrs. Mompesson   Few scenes could have been more painful than that of the young Rector standing at the grave of his wife.

Shortly after the outbreak of plague, Katherine Mompesson had tried to persuade her husband to leave the village for the sake of their two children— George and Elizabeth. Torn betwixt devotion to his family and duty to his flock, Mompesson had begged his wife to accompany the children to some place of safety, whilst he remained to help and counsel the harrassed people. Realising that her husband was determined to stay, and that no argument nor entreaty would persuade him otherwise, she herself had refused to leave and remained inflexible to all his appeals that she should consider her personal safety as well as the welfare of the children. So, with many tender caresses and anxious solicitations, the parents had taken leave of their children who were sent to be cared for by relatives in Yorkshire.

Thus the mother had remained in a home made lonely by the absence of her little family, that she might succour her husband in his ministry of mercy. The sound of prattling voices and the patter of young feet no longer echoed through the Rectory. Books and toys were stacked away and the nursery was still and empty. One of Elizabeth's childhood books, bereft of its covers and bearing the childish caligraphy: 'Elz. Mompesson—her book' was preserved at the Rectory.

Unsparing in her devotion to all, Mrs. Mompesson showed the utmost solicitude for her husband's welfare, with little regard for her own delicate state of health, for she herself suffered from pulmonary tuberculosis—a complaint which gave ample cause for concern.

Whenever he was able to escape from the pressures of making wills, dispensing medicines and carrying out the manifold duties of his vocation, the Rector often walked with his wife in the fields behind the rectory, not only finding personal relaxation, but hoping that the exercise would be of benefit to Mrs. Mompesson's health. One morning in August they were returning from this customary walk, when a sudden exclamation from his wife chilled the heart of the young clergyman.

'Oh, Mompesson, the air! how sweet it smells!'

Grim forebodings numbed his senses, denying him words with which to make immediate reply, for he realised that she—his greatest source of comfort and inspiration—had fallen victim to the plague. He well knew that this sweetness was not the whispered fragrance of wild flowers in the meadow, nor yet the scent of newly mown hay borne upon the morning breeze. He knew that this was the cruel deception of death. Finding an evasive reply to her unexpected words, Mompesson suggested that they should return home where his fears were soon fully confirmed.

Scarcely able to disguise his sorrow, the Rector nursed his wife with tender affection in spite of her remonstrances and repeated desire that she should be isolated from him. Calling her maid to the bedside, the sick mistress apologised for any harsh word or impetuous rebuke she may have administered. Although at times delirious in her speech, she occasionally repeated the pathetic cry: 'One drop of my Saviour's blood to save my soul from sin.' Under the impression that his wife's mental powers were weakened by suffering, the Rector catechised her at intervals from the Prayer Book but was convinced by each rational reply that she had received the assurance of pardoned sin. This knowledge gave him some measure of consolation. Gradually her strength ebbed away, and she again solicited her husband's prayers, responding to each petition with an audible 'Amen.'

After she had relapsed into silence, Mompesson enquired, 'My dear, dost thou mind?' to which she quietly replied in the affirmative and thus her lips were sealed in death.

> Ah! then Mompesson felt
> What human tongue nor poet's pen must feign—
> Quick to the grave the kindred earth was given;
> With e'en affection's last sad pledge foregone,
> The mortal kiss—for round those blighted lips,
> Exhaled the lingering spirit of the pest,
> As if in triumph o'er all that was once
> So lovely and beloved.
>
> (DR. HOLLAND).

This was a blow almost too heavy for Mompesson to endure, yet he realised that his bereavement was the catholic experience of all who had shared in this common fellowship of grief, and after the interment he resumed his pastoral duties with the same consideration he had always shown to his flock. How sadly he must have entered the name of the 200th victim in his diary of death:

'1666. Aug. 25. Bur: Katharin ye wife of Mr. William Mompefson.'

Mompesson's Letters The text of several letters written by the Rector during this time of intense physical and emotional stress, has been preserved. As they are printed in the works of Ebenezer Rhodes, William Wood, and other writers, the letters do not appear to be exact copies of the originals, but have obviously been edited by some self-appointed monitor before publication. Words have been deliberately altered and sentences omitted. The author has been at considerable trouble to try and present an accurate version of each letter, and the variances will be noted by readers sufficiently interested to make a comparative study with the censored copies of earlier days.

The original letter to Mompesson's children appears to be lost and the version published in John Holland's poem, *The Village of Eyam* (1821) has been adopted here as a genuine copy. The letter to Sir George Savile is an actual transcription —avoiding certain contractions and the use of the long 's'—from the original preserved in the Chatsworth archives. The first half of the Beilby letter is transcribed direct from an old document, but, unfortunately, the second half is missing and the author has reverted to the censored edition for its completion. Referring to these touching epistles, William and Mary Howitt wrote: 'In the whole range of literature we know nothing more pathetic than these letters.' The one addressed to his children contains the sad news of their mother's death.

"Eyam, August 31, 1666.

"Dear Hearts,

This brings you the doleful news of your dearest mother's death; the greatest loss that could befall you. I am deprived of a kind and loving consort, and you are bereaved of the most indulgent mother that ever poor little children had. But we must comfort ourselves in God, with this consideration—the loss is only ours; our sorrow is her gain, which should sustain our drooping spirits. I assure myself that her rewards and her joys are unutterable. Dear children, your dearest mother lived a holy life, and made a comfortable end, though by means of the sore pestilence, and she is now invested with a crown of righteousness.

"My children, I think it may be useful to have a narrative of your mother's virtues, that the knowledge thereof may teach you to imitate her excellent qualities. In the first place, let me recommend to you her piety and devotion, which were according to the exact principles of the church of England. In the next place, I can assure you, she was composed of modesty and humility, which virtues did possess her dear soul in a most exemplary manner. Her discourse was ever grave and meek, yet pleasant also; a vaunting and immodest word was never heard to come out of her mouth. Again, I can set out in her two other virtues, with no little confidence, viz. charity and frugality. She never valued anything she had, when the necessities of a poor neighbour did require it, but had a bountiful spirit towards all distressed and indigent persons;—yet she was never lavish or profuse, but carefully, constantly, and commendably frugal. She never liked the company of tattling women, and abhorred the wandering custom of going from house to house, thus wastefully spending of precious time, for she was ever busied in useful occupations. Yet, though thus prudent, she was always kind and affable; for, while she avoided those whose company could not instruct or benefit her, and would not unbosom herself to any such, she dismissed and avoided them with civility.

"I do believe, my dear hearts, upon sufficient grounds, that she was the kindest wife in the world, and think, from my soul, that she loved me ten times better than she did herself; for she not only resisted my entreaties, that she would fly with you, dear children, from this place of death, but, some few days before it pleased God to visit my house, she perceived a green matter to come from the issue in my leg, which she fancied a symptom that the distemper, raging amongst us, had gotten a vent that way, from whence she assured herself that I was passed the malignity of the disease, whereat she rejoiced exceedingly, amidst all the danger with which her near approach to me was attended, whom she believed to be infected.

"Now I will tell you my thoughts of this business. I think she was mistaken in the nature of that discharge which she saw; certainly it was the salve that made it look so green; yet her rejoicing on that account was a strong testimony of her love to me; for it is clear she cared not for her own peril, so I were safe.

"Further, I can assure you, my sweet babes, that her love to you was little inferior to that which she felt for me; since why should she thus ardently desire my longer continuence in this world of sorrows, but that you might have the comfort and protection of my life? You will imagine with what delight she used to talk of you both, and the pain that she took when you sucked your milk from her breasts, is almost incredible. She gave a strong testimony of her love for you, when she lay upon her death-bed. A few hours before she expired, I brought her some cordials, which she plainly told me she was not able to take. I entreated she would take them, for your dear sakes. At the mention of your names, she, with difficulty, lifted herself up and took them, which was to let me understand, that, while she had any strength left she would embrace an opportunity of testifying her affection to you.

"Now I will give you an exact account of the manner of her death. It is certain she had, for some time, had symptons of a consumption, and her flesh was considerably wasted thereby. However, being surrounded with infected families, she doubtless got the distemper from them. Her natural strength being impaired, she could not struggle with the disease, which made her illness so very short. Upon being seized, she shewed much contrition for the errors of her life, and often cried out,—'One drop of my Saviour's blood, to save my soul!'

"At the beginning of her sickness, she earnestly desired me not to come near her, lest I should receive harm thereby; but I can assure you I did not desert her, but, thank God, stood to my resolution not to leave her in sickness, who had been so tender a nurse to me in her health. Blessed be God, that he enabled me to be so helpful and consoling to her, for which she was not a little thankful. No worldly business was, during her illness, any disturbance to her! for she only minded making her calling and election sure: and she asked pardon of her maid-servant for having sometimes given her an angry word. I gave her several sweating antidotes, which had no kind operation, but rather scalded and inflamed her more, whereupon her dear head was distempered, which put her upon many incoherencies. I was much troubled thereat, and propounded several questions in divinity, as by whom, and upon what account, she expected salvation, and what assurances she had of the certainty thereof. Though in all other things she talked at random, yet, to these religious questions, she gave me as rational and welcome answers as I could desire; and at those times I bade her repeat after me certain prayers and ejaculations, which she always did with much devotion, which was no little comfort and admiration to me, that God should be so good and gracious to her.

"A little before her dear soul departed, she desired me to pray with her again. I went to her, and asked her how she did? Her answer was, that she was but looking when the good hour should come. Thereupon we went to prayers, and she made her responses from the Common Prayer-book as perfectly as if she had been in perfect health, and an amen to every pathetic expression. When we had ended our prayers for the visitation of the sick, we made use of those out of the Whole Duty of Man! and when I heard her say nothing, I urged,—'My dear, dost thou mind?' She answered 'Yes', and it was the last word she spoke.

"I question not, my dear hearts, that the reading of this account will cause many a salt tear to spring from your eyes; yet let this comfort you,—your dear mother is now a saint in heaven. I could have told you of many more of her excellent virtues; but I hope you will not in the least question my testimony, if in a few words, I tell you that she was pious and upright in all her conversation.

"Now, to that most blessed God, who bestowed upon her all those graces, be ascribed all honour, glory and dominion, the just tribute of all created beings, for evermore!

Amen!

"WILLIAM MOMPESSON"

One puzzling feature of the above text concerns the paragraph where Mompesson was summoned to his wife's death-bed, and is the omission of the statement printed in parenthesis in the edited version '(I was gone to bed)' and 'got up' later in the same sentence. It scarcely seems feasible that this could be an interpolation intruded by the editor, and equally unlikely that it would be deliberately expunged from Dr. Holland's version.

'The Saddest Letter' A further letter written to his patron, Sir George Savile, reveals the hopelessness of the Rector's plight, but expresses his willingness to pay the supreme sacrifice demanded by the plague. Death seemed inevitable, so he made his will, appointed executors, and resigned himself to the providence of the God he had served so well. His anxiety for the future welfare of his children is most pathetic.

"Honoured and Dear Sir,

This is the saddest letter that ever my pen did write, the destroying angell having taken up his quarters within my habitation. My Dearest Dear is gone to her eternall rest, and is invested with the crown of righteousness, having made a most happy end: and had she loved her selfe as well as mee, she had fled from the pit of destruction with her sweet infants, and might have p'longed her dayes. But she was resolved to dye a martyr for my interest. My drooping spirits are much refreshed with her joyes, which I assure my selfe are unutterable. Sir this paper is to bid you a hearty farewell for ever and to bring you my humble thanks for all your noble favours, and I hope you will believe a dying man, that I have as much love as honor for you; and I will bend my feeble knees to the God of heaven, that you, my Dear Lady, and your children may be blest with externall, internall and eternall happinesse, and that the same blessings may fall upon my Lady Sunderland and her relations. Dear sir, let your dying Chaplain recommend this truth to you and your family. That noe happinesse, or solid comfort can be found in this vale of tears, like living a pious life. And pray retain this rule: Never do that thing upon which you dare not first ask a blessing of God, uppon the successe thereof. Sir I have made bold to name you in my will for an Executor, and I hope you will not take it ill, I have joyned others with you, that will take from you the trouble. Your favourable aspect, I know, will be a great comfort to my distressed Orphans. I am not desirous they may be great, but good, and my great request is that they may be brought up in the nurture and admonition of the Lord. I thank God, I am content to shake hands with all the World, and I have many comfortable assurances that God will accept mee upon the Account of his Son; And I find God moor good than ever I thought or imagined, and from my soul I wish that his goodness were not soe much abused and contemned. Sir I desire you would be pleased to make choice of a humble pious man to succeed me in this parsonage; and could I see your face before my departure hence, I could inform you which way I think he may live comfortably among these people, which would be some satisfaction to mee before I dye. Dear Sir, I beg your prayers and desire you to procure the prayers of those about you, that I may not be daunted by all the powers of hell; and that I may have dying graces, that when I come to dye, I may be found in a right dying posture. And with tears I begg that when you are praying for fatherlesse infants, that you would remember my two pretty babes. Sir pardon the rude style of this paper, and if my head be discomposed you cannot wonder at mee, however be pleased to believe that I am.

Dear Sir,

Your most obliged, most affectionate and gratefull servant,

WILLIAM MOMPESSON"

"Honoured Sir,

Mr. Mompesson did not write this, but dictated it to mee yesterday upon Eyam Moore, & desires you would be pleased to consider Mr. Wright, he having a very hard bargain of the Lott & Cope by reason of the infection, & sayes he would have bin silent in it, had he not mocioned Mr. Wright to it. A boy came from him this day, & told mee an imperfect story that he desired Mr. Gardner to send him some Cordiall spirits.

(Blessed be God) He is yet in good health. Soe rests

Your Worship's humble servant

JOHN: WALKER Vic.

Hathersage. September 2, 1666".

What scenes of desolation must have marked this time of unexampled mortality in the annals of the village? Where was the reaper to harvest the neglected crops? Both his scythe and sickle were flecked with rust and dull because of disuse. The cereals had ripened and rotted in the fields, or were devoured by starving cattle. The strong brown hands which in former years had guided the plough in springtime, and wielded the flail in autumn, had left their tasks unfinished. Just as the farms were empty and deserted, so the lead-mines were idle and forsaken. No longer the smell of powder and smoke lingered at the mouth of adit or shaft, or haunted the silent 'grooves.' Tools of wood and iron rotted or rusted away. The shining spoils of the groover's basket were no longer spilled into the washing tubs to be sieved and separated for sale to the lead-merchants. The creeping paralysis of plague had brought the industry to a standstill.

Marshall Howe Bereaved   An incident happend in August which awakened the sorrow and sympathy hitherto undiscovered in the character of Marshall Howe. Until then he had quite casually discharged his unenviable duties, but, when his wife Joan sickened and died, he became personally conscious of the grief endured by others. With greater care he prepared the place of mortal repose, and, after completing the work of interment, made his despondent way home to discover that his only son, William, had fallen victim to the plague and the charnel tools were again requisitioned to repeat the melancholy task as he shared the bitter cup in the sacrament of sorrow. Tender chords were touched by invisible fingers, awakening a distant response within the depths of his grief-scarred soul, as he filled in the trench containing the putrid body. That night a lonely man returned to a lonely home.

The time of the annual Wake passed by. No gaily dressed throng had gathered to celebrate the occasion; no choristers had taken their place in Church to commemorate its birthday with sacred anthems; no dancers swayed to and fro across the village green as rejoicing music roused echoes in the distant glades. The place which had so often witnessed the coronation of mirth was now deserted. And what must have been the thoughts of Rowland Torre whose wedding to Emmot had been planned for this day in August?

A story is recorded of a man living at the west end of the village who heard, one evening in late August, that his sister was ill of the plague. She was a widow and lived in the Lydgate. In spite of the awful risk, he was determined to visit her, and made the venture early next morning, only to find the tenantless home had been rifled by Marshall Howe who had buried the body in a grave dug in the garden. Returning home to relate the sad tidings to his wife, it soon became evident that he had contracted the plague. Within a few days the man, his wife, and all his family were numbered with the dead.

During September the sparsely peopled village was further depopulated. What an anniversary! There had been many changes since George Viccars had been buried twelve months before.

Cessation of Plague   Fourteen of the wretched remnant perished in October and with their disfigured bodies the plague itself was buried.

As the days dragged wearily by, and no sign of revived infection became apparent, the villagers concluded that the disease had worn itself out. Yet, before they were released from their enforced insularity, considerable work had to be done. Mompesson personally supervised the destruction of materials calculated to conceal germs and discouraged any inclination to parsimony by burning more of his own clothing than was actually necessary. Furniture, clothing and bedding were committed to the flames of huge bonfires, although the inventories of the goods of victims contain reference to amounts of bed linen, blankets and even wearing apparel. Houses visited by the disease were fumigated and reconditioned to make them habitable again. In the following letter to an uncle, Mompesson described the desolate condition of the village. As mentioned before, the first half of the letter has been transcribed from an old document copied by a possibly less literate person than the anonymous friend of the Rector to whom the original was dictated. A point of particular interest is the reference to 'burying' (not 'burning' as the edited version says) of goods. The letter is reproduced complete with spelling errors, to the point where the edited version takes over.

"To John Beilby Esq. in Yorkshire Transcribed at Middleton near Eyam, November 20, 1666.
Dear Sir,
I suppose this letter will seem to you no less than a Miracle that my Habitation is

inter vivos. I was loath to affright you with a paper from my Hand, therefore I made bold with a friend to Transcribe thies lines. I know you are sensible of my Condition and the loss of the kindest wife in the World whose life was truly imitable and her end most Comfortable. She was in an excellent posture when Death came with his Summons, which fills me with many Confident assurances that she is now invested with a Crown of Righteousness. I find that maxim verified by too sad experience, *bonum magis carendo quam fruendo cenitur*. Had I been so thankful as my Condition did deserve, I might yet have had my Dearest Deare in my bosom, but now farewell all happy days and God grant that I may repent my great ingatiude.—The Condition of this Place hath been so sad that I presuade my self it did exceed all History and Exhample; I may truly say our Town is become a GOLGOTHA, the Place of a skull, and had there not been a small remnant of us left, we had been as Sodom and like unto Gomorrah. My ears never heard such doleful lamentations, my nose never felt such horrid smells, and my eyes never beheld such gastly Spectacles. Here hath been 76 Families visited within my Parish, out of which have died 259. Blessed be God, all our fears are over, for none have died here of the infection since the Eleventh of October, besides we have not any one person under a Present Suspicion and all the pest Houses have been long empty.

"I intend (God willing) to spend most of this week in seeing all woollen Cloaths fumed and purified as well for the satisfaction as safety of the Country. Hear hath been such burying of goods, that the like (I think) was never known and indeed in this I think we have been too precise; for my own part I have scarce left my self apparel to shelter my Body from the Cold and have wasted more than needed, merely for Exhample. As to my own condition I can't say that I ever had better Health during this Dreadfull visitation, neither can I say that I have had any Symptoms of the Disease. My man had the Distemper and upon the appearance of a Tumor I applied several Chymical Antidotes which had a very kind operation and with ye Blessing of God kept the venom from the Heart and after the rising broke, he was very well . . . My Maid continued in health, which was a blessing; for had she quailed, I should have been ill set to have washed and gotten my provisions. I know I have had your prayers, and I conclude that the prayers of good people have rescued me from the jaws of death. Certainly I had been in the dust had not Omnipotence itself been conquered by holy violence.

"I have largely tasted of the goodness of the Creator and the grim looks of death did ever affright me. I always had a firm faith that my babes would do well, which made me willing to shake hands with the unkind, froward world, yet I shall esteem it a mercy if I am frustrated in the hopes I had of a translation to a better place, and God grant that with patience I may wait for my change, and that I may make a right use of His mercies; as the one hath been tart, so the other hath been sweet and comfortable.

"I perceive by a letter from Mr. Newby of your concern for my welfare. I make no question but I have your unfeigned love and affection. I assure you that during my troubles you have had a great deal of room in my thoughts. Be pleased, dear Sir, to accept the presentments of my kind respects, and impart them to your good wife and all my dear relations. I can assure you that a line from your hand will be welcome to your sorrowful and affectionate nephew.

WILLIAM MOMPESSON."

Vanished Monuments Many places of interment were marked by stones for a number of years, but some of these have since been removed and desecrated to ignoble uses. They were recognised as useful material with which to pave houses, barns or pathways, and some have been hollowed and worn by many feet until the inscriptions are now illegible. The Miners' Arms croft was an unofficial cemetery and formerly contained a number of rude stone slabs to record the solemn fact. For many years amusement caterers pitched their caravans on this site and transformed the erstwhile burial ground into an annual fairground. One stone to the memory of Alice Wragg was mentioned by Wood as serving as a paving-stone in the parlour of a house opposite the Church, and this was rediscovered beneath the floor of the former Post Office when sewerage excavations were being made in 1963. Two dating errors, however, suggest that it may have been discarded as a memorial owing to these mistakes, and it also appears to have been bisected from a twin stone. Wood also refers to two or three which existed in the Delph to the memory of the Wraggs; one or two behind the old almshouses which belonged to a family named Whiteley; and another inscribed 'Bridget Talbot', Ano. Dom. 1666', then in a cabinet of curios at Derby. This was obviously the Bridget to whom reference has been made. The crumbling remains of a tomb in the Delph inspired Richard Furness to write a poem entitled *The Tomb of the Valley*, of which he says in a footnote: 'About fifty years since I saw some of its remains. It was similar to the one still standing at Roylee; but has perished.'

> Ah! There no more
> The green graves of the pestilence are seen;
> O'er them the plough hath pass'd and harvests wave,
> Where haste and horror flung th' infectious corse.
>
> (EBENEZER ELLIOTT).

Plague Register   The list of victims in the Parish Register is prefaced with: *September, 1665. Here followeth ye names with ye numbers of ye persons who died of ye plague.* The last interment on Nov. 1, 1666, is numbered 260 and the person thus distinguished was *Abraham, ye son of John Mortin defunct.*

The original Registers dating from 1630 to 1705 consisted of separate documents, and were replaced with a copy transcribed by the Rev. Joseph Hunt. This rector, after baptizing a sick child at the Miners' Arms, was foolishly involved in a mock marriage with the landlord's daughter, Anne Fearn. The resulting scandal was brought to the notice of the bishop of the diocese who insisted that the marriage should be legally confirmed. Unfortunately Hunt was already engaged to a lady of some social status and she sued him for breach of promise. Reduced to poverty by litigation expenses, the young clergyman was compelled to take sanctuary in the Church in order to avoid the bailiffs seeking his arrest. He there lived with his wife in a vestry specially built for their accommodation, and in this building both their children were born. In addition to discharging his ecclesiastical duties, he beguiled the weary hours by re-writing the registers. Both he and his wife lie buried in the vestry where they had made their home and where their family had been born.

Inventories   Several inventories of the goods of plague victims have also come to light and these reflect, not only the care exercised by the executors in discharging their responsibilities, but give some indication of contemporary values. For example, out of an estate valued in total at £50, Rowland Mower's stock of 'cooper wood made and unmade' was assessed at £22 8s. 6d. His two horses were valued at £2 10s; two cows and a heifer at £5 and five sheep at £1.

Corn and hay was estimated to be worth £3, and his bed, clothes and linen were valued at the same figure. The value placed on Rowland's pewter and brass, which no doubt included flagons, dishes and tableware, was £2.

The inventory of Richard Talbot's goods will suffice as an example.

"A Just and True Inventory of all the Goods and Chattles Moveable and immoveable Quick and dead of Richard Talbott of Ryley in the parish of Eyam in the County of Darby Husbandman Deceased the 22nd day of July 1666.

	£	s.	d.
His purse and Apparell	5	0	0
Fourscore & seaventeene sheepe	23	0	0
five cowes 2 bullocks, 2 oxen & two heifors	23	0	0
three horses	10	0	0
his Corne and hay	26	0	0
A Swine	1	2	0
his pewter and Brafs	4	10	0
a waine carts plowes harowes yoaks teams horse geares and husbandry ware	4	0	0
Seaven stone of wool	3	0	0
A Garner & three Chests	1	13	6
foure paire of Bed stocks	2	10	0
one Ark & a Cubbord	1	10	0
Two tables A hingboard & a forme	0	10	0
three chaires & stooles	0	6	0
tubs, Loomes & Kitts	1	0	0
three spinninge wheeles	0	4	0
Boards & pieces of timber	1	0	0
Iron tooles of severall sorts	1	0	0
a salting kimnell & A ffatt	0	10	0
a paire of Cart legs a hackney sadle 3 shovels	0	10	0
A silver spoone	0	5	0
Linen yarne	1	10	0
his Maynor	1	10	0
Corne sacks & oat bags	0	10	0
A hive of Bees & two quarts of hony	0	15	0
Ffoure strike & a halfe of meale	0	15	0
A Bed Coveringe a Coverlitt a paire of blankits & A Chafs bed	5	0	0
A paire of sheets pillow beers table napkins with other linnens	4	0	0
A bible & a fafsgard	0	10	0
A Muskett a fword a Iron Candlestick	0	11	6
A Landiron Rackets tongs pot hooks with other necessary things	0	10	0
For any thing thats forgotten	0	5	0
	126	7	0

Godfrey Torre
  his marke
Robert Slinne   **Robert Heild**
  his marke

Another interesting document concerning this family has come into the author's possession, and suggests that the smithy at Riley had been recently erected on land purchased in 1662 by Thomas Talbot (father, uncle or brother of Richard?) from George Wragg, an Eyam lead-miner. An abridged extract reads: 'This Indenture made Sep. 24th in the 14th Carolus II (1662) between George Ragge of Eyam, myner, of the one part, and Thomas Talbott of Ryeley in the parish of Eyam of the other part, WITNESSETH, that for the sum of twenty five shillings . . . George Ragge hath sold to the said Thomas Talbott, his heirs and assigns for ever . . . all that Gardensteed lying at the east end of the dwelling house of the said George Ragge, and now in the tenure and occupation of the said Thomas Talbott (whereupon he hath built a smithy) . . .

George Ragge
his mark

Sealed and delivered in the presence
of Thomas   Bray
      David   Cowlishaw
  and John   Chapman
      his mark.

Commemoration Service On the last Sunday in August (Wakes Sunday) a service is held at Cucklet Church, when numerous pilgrims visit this mecca of the Derbyshire mountains to pay homage to the memory of the plague martyrs. The first commemorative sermon was preached by the Rev. Thomas Seward a century after the Plague. On the occasion of the bi-centenary, three sermons were preached, and in 1965 the preacher was the Archbishop of York, Dr. D. Coggan, now Archbishop of Canterbury. The service has been held as an annual event since 1905.

Civilisation—if one may be pardoned a personal reflection—has cause to be grateful that this most destructive weapon in the arsenal of death has been rendered so ineffective by the painstaking researches of medical science. We need to salute those who have dedicated their lives to the tedious conquest of disease. In the laboratory men have quitely experimented, still persisting in spite of frequent failure, until they found the cause and perfected the cure of this and other dread diseases which have afflicted mankind.

Revival of the Plague? Two records are extant concerning minor epidemics of disease which, at the time, were suspected of being revivals of the Plague. Miss Anna Seward wrote:-

"In the summer of 1757, five cottagers were digging on the heathy mountain above Eyam, which was the place of graves after the churchyard became too narrow a repository. The men came to something which had the appearance of once having been linen. Conscious of their situation, they instantly buried it again. In a few days they all sickened of a putrid fever, and three of the five died. The disorder was contagious and proved mortal to numbers of the inhabitants. My father, who was the Canon of Lichfield, resided in that city with his family, at the period when the subtle, unextinguished, though much abated power of the most dreadful of all diseases awakened from the dust in which it had slumbered ninety-one-years."

Referring to the same circumstance, Dr. Holland says that the five men were digging amongst the plague graves when they came to something which had the appearance of *lime* (not linen). Three of them died and the spreading disease 'proved mortal to seventy persons.' Quicklime was used in the interment of the uncoffined corpses. But William Wood commented: 'Tradition knows nothing of the matter and the mortality of that year was only ordinary. Miss Seward was undoubtedly misinformed.' And so this suspected revival remains something of a mystery.

Wood himself mentions a further epidemic during the summer of 1779 when

"A putrid fever prevailed in Eyam and the following individuals died in a short time of the malignant disease: William Baxter, Elias Vicars, Robert Dooley, Elizabeth Unwin, Robert Unwin, Mary Benson, George Bradley, Ann Sheldon, Samuel Brittlebank, Elizabeth Benson, Isaac Benson, Thomas Bradshaw, George Chapman, Mary Wyatt, James Mortin, Ann Timperley, and Ann Rowbottom. Those who died swelled in the neck and groin; and the villagers apprehended that the ghost of the plague had risen from the dust".

Brief Biographies of Rectors By way of concluding this summary of the momentous thirteen months when about 267 of those who had remained in Eyam were massacred so swiftly, it seems fitting to supply a few details concerning the Rev. Thomas Stanley and the Rev. William Mompesson. There is an Old Testament record of warriors engaged in continuous battle until every man's hand clave to the hilt of his sword. This was the type of warfare waged by these two men. Theirs was an unceasing struggle, day and night, with little respite, rest or relaxation. And it must seem rather invidious to the liberal-minded reader that, largely owing to former religious prejudice and intolerance, one of these brave men should be virtually canonised while the other has been the victim of ostracism and misrepresentation. Although post-mortem appreciation is the only tribute we may pay, it seems a reproach to reason that bigotry should have attempted the suppression even of this. Yet, it is affirmed that a mural tablet, erected in Church to Stanley's memory, was reversed to the wall by order of one of his successors. This slight to his memory has since been rescinded by the generous and broad-minded action of a sympathetic clergyman who had the present stone erected against the chancel wall to record the work and worth of this great man.

Stanley's claims to distinction have been somewhat naturally overshadowed by the well deserving tributes paid to Mompesson, and our instinctive sympathy goes to the latter in the loss of his young and devoted wife. But one feels that he himself would have been nauseated by any attempt to make capital out of his own exemplary conduct during Eyam's hour of tragedy in order to weight the scales against Stanley, or to discredit his sincere convictions on ecclesiastical policy; convictions which were so strong that he suffered expulsion from his chosen career and alienation from former friends who did not share his scruples and opinions. His loyalty to conscience contrasted sharply with that of his immediate predecessor and successor, the Rev. Shorland Adams, who avowed that rather than surrender his living 'he would have sworn the crow was white.' Therefore it seems regrettable that there has been an increasing tendency to prefix the name of Mompesson with other landmarks than the hillside well,

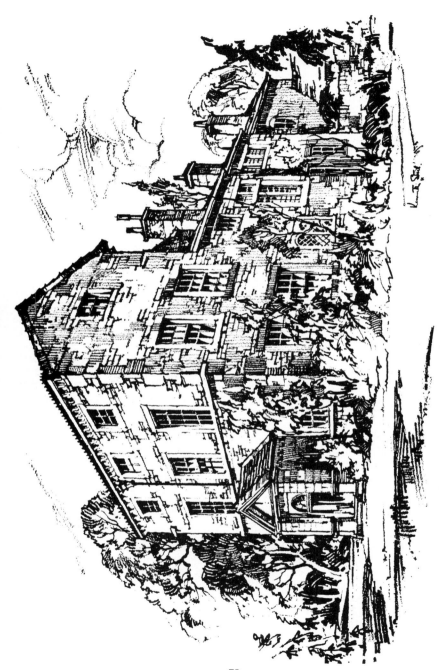

EYAM RECTORY—*Drawing by Kenneth Steel is produced by courtesy of Davy-Ashmore Limited, Sheffield.*

including the 17th century portion of the rectory; its study and staircase, and even the church pulpit.

Even in his own day Stanley was unpopular with a section of the village community because of his nonconformist beliefs, and this element showed its intolerance by agitating to effect his ejection from Eyam. In his *Spiritualibis Pecci*, the Rev. William Bagshaw says:- 'When he could not serve his people publicly, he was helpful to them in private. Some persons yet alive will testify how helpful he was to his people when the pestilence prevailed in Eyam, that he continued with them when, as it is written, 259 persons of ripe age and 58 children were cut off thereby. When some who might have been better employed moved the then Earl of Devonshire, Lord Lieutenant, to remove him out of the town, I am told by the creditable that he said: 'It was more reasonable that the whole country should in more than words testify their thankfulness to him who, together with the care of the town, had taken such care *as no one else did*, to prevent the infection of the towns adjacent'.'

The fact that two-thirds of his former parishioners subscribed to support him after his ejection from the Established Church, is a further tribute to the esteem in which he was held in the village where he had so diligently laboured as legal, medical and spiritual counsellor.

Thomas Stanley was born at Duckmanton, near Chesterfield, and the arms of his family may be seen carved over the entrance to a house in this village. A public-house still bears the name of 'Stanley Arms'. Educated at Netherthorpe Grammar School, Staveley, he entered St. John's College, Cambridge, and took the degree of M.A. at the age of 22 years. He was first employed in a tutorial capacity to a family and later began his church ministry at Handsworth, following which he spent three years at Dore and eight at Ashford-in-the-Water before coming to Eyam in 1644. He filled the vacancy created when the Rev. Shorland Adams was deprived (because of his royalist support during the Civil War) of the livings of Eyam and Treeton, Yorkshire, which he had held in plurality.

An interesting 'humble petition and certificate' (undated) was addressed by the freeholders and other inhabitants of Eyam to Sir George Savile about 1661-2 and stated: 'Humbly shewing and declaringe that one Shorland Adams about twenty years since was minister at Eyam aforesaid and that duringe the tyme hee continued as minister there your petitioners well knows and humbly certifie that the said Mr. Adams was scandalous in life, negligent and idle in preachinge, of a turbulent and Contentious spirit and proud behaviour, to our great prejudice and discouragement; with all of which your honourable father was well acquainted and declared himselfe much displeased with the Carriage and Course of life of the said Mr. Adams, for which Cause and for that the said Mr. Adams then held and enjoyed the parsonage of Treeton in the County of Yorke, the said Mr. Adams shortly afterwards left Eyam, and being then destitute of a minister, through the mercy of God, and assistance of our friends, we procured one Mr. Thomas Stanley an able, peaceable pyous orthodox Devine to be our minister, who hath Continued with us ever since and Diligently Carefully and Constantly hath preached and taught amongst us, by whose pyous preachinge and painefull instruction wee have received much comfort to our Soules, and by the good Example of his holy and peaceable life are much encouraged.

'Wherefore wee humbly beseech your honour (beinge informed that it is in your power only) to Continue and settle the said Mr. Stanley to be our minister at Eyam aforesaid and thereby you will bring much glory to God and Comfort to our Soules, and for which wee shall ever prayse God and pray for your honour's happiness.'

The document was attested by the signatures of 69 parishioners, a number of whom died of the plague.

After Shorland Adams had been reinstated in 1660, Stanley is thought to have acted as curate until St. Bartholomew's Day, 1662, when he was expelled or resigned from the Established Church. After leaving the village for a short time, he returned and was supported by the generosity of many of his former parishioners. The death of his devoted wife was a source of great grief to him. She was buried at Eyam on June 14th, 1664. Stanley himself died on the eighth anniversary of his deposition from the living, and, although he was not allowed to conduct the interment service, the Rev. William Bagshaw (Apostle of the Peak) preached a funeral sermon in his memory, choosing the combined verses of Zechariah ch. 1, v. 5, and Isaiah ch. 57, v. 1 for his text. He paid the following tribute to Stanley:

"His diligence in studying, and his zeal in sound, plain, practical preaching were worthy of (what they met with) a remark . . . He was a great encourager of week-day lectures, by his preaching at 'em and by his presence when his Juniors or Seniors preached . . . He was a very visible and audible confutor of those who venture to deny free conceived prayer, adventuring to say there is no such gift . . . "

Relating the circumstances of his friend's death, Bagshaw wrote:

"Poor I was on a Sabbath night called out of my bed (as I remember) to visit him whom I found in a desirable frame of spirit, tho' weak in body, as I also found that, tho' on account of his Nonconformity he had suffered much, he rejoiced that he suffered in (and for) that cause. Within three days, even on St. Bartholomew's Day (still called black), he expired".

It is of interest to note that Thomas Stanley had at least one son. His name was John and he was educated at Tideswell Grammar School (founded in 1579 by Bishop Pursglove), and later at the same college as his father, St. John's, Cambridge. He was appointed to the staff of the Grammar School and in 1678 deputised as Headmaster for John Rowarth who had obtained 'a special license to absent himself in order that he might take a degree at the University of Cambridge.'

William Mompesson was born in 1637 or 8, and was descended from a family of French extraction residing at Bathampton in Wiltshire. The family arms are described in heraldic phraseology as: '*Argent a Lion rampant sable charged on the shoulder with a martlet of the field. Crest, a jug or with a string azure, tasselled of the first. Motto: "Ma joy en dieu seulement."* ' He married as his first wife, Katherine Carr of Cocken in Durham. In a letter written from Rufford on May 22nd, 1661, Sir George Savile was notified by his agent, William Kirk, that 'Mr. Mompesson since he came to Welley (possibly known to you) hath marryed a wife, who is now coming hither to be with him.' Before coming to Eyam in April, 1664, he held an appointment at Scalby, near Scarborough, where the list of incumbents includes 'Wm. Mompesson, clerk, afterwards Rector of Eyam, Derbys,' and is dated 1662-3. He had two children, George and Elizabeth, at the time.

In his work on *Lazarettos,* John Howard wrote:-

"I am here reminded of a singular fact which I gladly mention in honour to the memory of a worthy character: when the plague raged in London, 1665, the infection was conveyed by means of a parcel of clothes to the remote village of Eyam in the Peak of Derbyshire. In this place it broke out in September, 1665, and continued its ravages upwards of a year, when 260 persons died of it. The worthy Rector, Mr. Mompesson, whose name may rank with those of Cardinal Bonower, of Milan, or the good Bishop of Marseilles, at its breaking out, resolved not to quit his parishioners, but used every argument to prevail with his wife to leave the infected place."

Three years after the Plague, Mompesson was appointed to the living of Eakring in Nottinghamshire, and there humoured the apprehensive people by living in a hut in Rufford Park until they were satisfied that he was immune from infection. He was also refused the pulpit of the church and preached beneath an ash tree which became known as 'Pulpit Ash', and when it fell victim to a gale, a stone cross was erected by Lord Savile to identify the site. It was cleaned in 1965 by Eakring Parish Council and a path made to provide easier access for the public. A sapling ash has also been planted at the spot.

In his *The Plague of Eyam: A Tercentenary Re-evaluation,* Mr. G. R. Batho sought to discredit and dismiss this well established belief with the weak claim that the Eakring services were held in the open-air while the church was being restored. The only evidence offered in support of this theory was a letter written by Mompesson in 1672 seeking financial help for the project from his patron who had now been made Viscount Halifax. This argument has little validity; its three main weaknesses being that (1) it is scarcely feasible the congregation would be expected to walk nearly half a mile out of the village for temporary services which (2) would hardly have been held in the open because of possible inclement weather, and (3) a subsequent patron of the living would never have gone to the expense of erecting a memorial to mark the temporary closure of the church.

On one occasion, Mompesson was publicly slighted by his patron after he had made a flattering speech in which he invoked the blessing of Heaven upon the knight. Sir George rebuked the speaker by acidly replying that even if he could not help being a fool, there was no need to inform the Almighty whose fool he was. Yet in December, 1666, Sir George had praised Mompesson for his heroism in a letter written from London:- 'I am very glad to hear the sickness is leaving you at Eyam, which is not to be attributed to anything more than your care, excepting God Almighty's mercy to a place that hath been so long afflicted: you have been as much a Martyr all this while, as if you had died for your flock, having, besides your hazard, sacrificed the pleasure of your life to your duty for which you ought to have the reward of an eternal esteem from all good people.'

Mompesson married a widow, Mrs. Charles Newby, by whom he had two daughters and two sons who died in infancy. He was honoured by several ecclesiastical appointments. These included the Prebends of Southwell and York, together with the offered Deanery of Lincoln: this latter was declined in favour of his friend, Dr. Fuller. Incidentally, few people who admire Chantrey's 'Sleeping Children' in Lichfield Cathedral, are aware that the two sisters— Ellen Jane and Marianne Robinson—were the great, great, great, great grand-children of William Mompesson. An oil painting of Mompesson is preserved at Southwell Minster and another is in the possession of the Graves Art Gallery at Sheffield, although this may be a portrait of his son, George, who was Rector of Barnborough, Yorkshire. A gold-framed miniature has also been presented to Eyam Church and was in the custody of the Rector, Rev. E. M. Turner.

Claims have been made concerning other mementoes. At Cheltenham a carved oak settle—bearing the names of William and Katherine Mompesson—was offered to the village, but the required price precluded a purchase being made. It is reasonable to speculate that this piece of furniture may have been companion to the chair in Eyam Church which was acquired from a Liverpool antique shop by Canon E. Hacking, a former rector of Eyam. A striped glass, formerly displayed in the museum of Poole's Cavern, Buxton, purported to be a personal possession of Mompesson, and was claimed to have held vinegar in which coins were washed during the Plague. Along with other exhibits, the glass was stolen from the museum during a raid made by thieves.

It may also be mentioned that, in connection with the Mompesson family, Salisbury Cathedral has a proud monument to Sir Richard Mompesson and his wife, Dame Katherine. Erected about the beginning of the 17th century, the memorial has been beautifully restored by the Friends of Salisbury Cathedral. Although it has the exaggerated detail of that period, and has various heraldic quarterings, one cannot but admire its impressive dignity. Winchester Cathedral has a memorial to Elizabeth Mompesson, and this is neighbour to the tomb of Isaac Walton, the renowned angler. Tedworth in Wiltshire has an interesting story of John Mompesson, a local magistrate, who committed to prison a beggar musician, confiscating his drum. This resulted in strange supernatural happenings which began with the drum beating outside the windows of his house and later indoors. Visitors to Mompesson House in the Cathedral Close at Salisbury will see the incident recalled in the decor of the finely painted panels of the entrance hall. This interesting mansion is a property administered by the National Trust and is another link with the Mompesson family.

William Mompesson died on March 7th, 1708, and was buried in Eakring Church where a stained glass window and a brass shield inscribed in Latin perpetuate his memory. Miss Anna Seward wrote: 'His memory ought never to die! it should be immortal as the spirit that made it worthy to live.'

Two Derby Heroes   There is little doubt that other clergy and laymen played an equally heroic part to that of Mompesson and Stanley when placed in com-parable circumstances, and although the Biblical phrase 'there name liveth for evermore' may not be as applicable to them, yet they too could be described as 'not having counted their lives dear unto them' in the face of similar peril.

And while it is true that many unfaithful shepherds did desert their flocks, yet there were others who died while attempting to relieve the sick and dying. This is attested by the fact that two-thirds of the benefices of Derbyshire were dispossessed of their clergy in 1349—a fairly positive proof of their fidelity and faith.

One worthy who survived the perils of plague was the nonconforming Rev. John Crompton of All Hallows, Derby. It is recorded that 'Mr. Crompton gained much respect at Derby by his cheerful and obliging temper, but particularly by continuing to perform all the duties of his office during the time of a raging pestilence, by which the town was so desolate that grass sprung up in the market-place. Yet he himself was preserved from the infection, which he attributed to the blessing of God on a plaster applied to his stomach by an able physician . . . '

At the Restoration he was forced to surrender his living, although 'his countenance was much desired, and a certificate was drawn up testifying his worth and loyalty, subscribed by several aldermen and some substantial inhabitants of Derby, as well as ministers of the town and places adjacent, but it had no effect.' He ministered at Arnold, Notts., until the Act of Uniformity when he was dispossessed of his living. One of his sons, Samuel, was minister of a dissenting congregation at Doncaster, while his grandson of the same name was an eminent banker in Derby, founding the company which later became Crompton and Evans.

Another of Derby's unsung heroes of plague days was Richard Croshawe, a Dick Whittington who was the son of a poor Derby nailer and set off in his leather doublet to seek his fortune in London where, by industry and perseverance, he acquired a fortune of £10,000. His success story is recorded in All Saints' Church, Derby, and speaks of: 'Richard Croshawe, of London, esq., sometyme Mr. of the Right Worshipfull Compane of Goldsmiths and Deputie of Broad Streete Ward, a man pious, and liberall to the poor, in the great plague 1625, neglecting his own saftie aboade in the citie to provide for their reliefe . . . ' He is represented in the memorial holding his nailer's hammer.

In London we are told of an ejected Rev. Thomas Vincent who remained in the city and preached from pulpits deserted by the beneficed clergy. He afterwards published one of the best accounts of the city's grim story. A less noble story is told in a Latin inscription in All Saints' at Derby and concerned Sir William and Lady Elizabeth Wheeler who, having fled from London to avoid the pestilence, were remorselessly pursued and overtaken by the disease at Derby in 1666.

John Flamsteed, the first Astronomer Royal, is stated by some writers to have been born at Derby in 1646 and taken by his parents to Denby to escape the plague, but Stephen Glover says that he was born at Denby Hall.

Conclusion Such is the story of the most melancholy and yet momentous year in the life of Eyam. It is a story which has thrilled succeeding generations and made the village a shrine of pilgrimage. Ever increasing numbers have become familiar with the tragic—but triumphant—story of a shrinking community of ordinary people who accepted voluntary isolation, facing the possibility of extinction that they might protect neighbouring townships from suffering the horrors of disease, death and desolation which had become their everyday experience.

The courage and self-sacrifice revealed in this 17th century story remains as a challenge to our own and all succeeding generations. It should widen our outlook and broaden our vision. It should help us to reject the attitude of introspection and help us look beyond the hills which environ our village, and venture beyond the shores of our native land. It should also make us grateful for the skill and devotion, tact and understanding of the 20th century medical profession; surgeons, doctors, nurses, research and ancillary workers who are ceaselessly engaged in the alleviation of suffering and distress, and in the conquest of the many diseases which afflict mankind.

The Riley Graves, Eyam

85

ADDENDUM

More Recipes against the Plague. From the Rector's Book of Clayworth, Notts. 'Take three pints of mus-cadine wine, boil it in a handful of Sage, as much rue, till a pint is wasted, then strain it, and set it on ye fire again, then put therein of long pepper, ginger and nutmegs, of each ye 3rd part of an ounce, beat all together into a fine powder, let it boil a little, then put therein 2 ounces of treacle, an ounce of Metrodate, and a quarter of a pint of Angelico water before you put them in. Take of it warm both morning and evening in your bed a spoonful or two, if infected, and sweat after it, but if not infected a spoonful a day is sufficient, half in ye morning, and half in ye evening, to prevent infection.'

Another recipe states: 'Take the inward Bark of the Ash Tree one Pound, of Walnut, with the green outward Shells, to the number of Fifty, cut these small: of Scabious, of Vervin, of each a Handful, of Saffron two Drams, pour upon these the strongest Vinegar you can get, four Pints, let them a little boil together upon a very soft fire, and then stand in a close Pot, well stopt all night upon the Embers. After distil them with a soft fire, and receive the Water close Kept. Give unto the Patient laid in Bed and well covered with Cloathes, two ounces of this water to drink, and let him be provoked to Sweat: and every eight hours (during the space of four and twenty Hours) give him the same quantity to drink.'

A further recipe prescribes 'An Ale Posset drunk with Pimpernel seethed in it, till it taste strong of it, drunk often, removes the infection, tho' it had reached the very heart.'

Further notes on Mompesson's family: In Canon Prior's Book on St. Peter's Church, Mansfield. 'One of William Mompesson's beautiful daughters, 15 years of age, was carried off from school at Doncaster, by John, Marquis of Granby (son of John, third Duke of Rutland). A sham marriage was performed, and they lived together as man and wife for some years, part of the time at Averham Park, then the property of a brother of the Marquis. They had a son who died early, and a daughter (Anne Manners) who afterwards became the wife of John Manners Sutton, of Kelham. Poor Mrs. Mompesson (as she was called) left the Marquis as soon as she was aware that she was not his wife, and went to her father's with her children, but he refused to receive her. She then determined to try whether her aunt, Mrs. Gilbert-Hall, of Kettlethorp, had not a warmer heart, and by her she was welcomed with every kindness.' This reference is to the grandson of William who distinguished himself during the Plague at Eyam and later became Rector of Eakring.

George Mompesson, son of William, was Vicar of Mansfield in 1700. He had married Alice, daughter of John Broomhead, of Laughton-en-le-Morthern, at Aston, Yorkshire, in 1689, and on leaving Mansfield he was appointed to the living of Barnborough which he held until his death in February, 1731. His son, William, succeeded him as Vicar of Mansfield, and he married Elizabeth Chappel at Blidworth Church the year he was appointed to the living. She was the grand-daughter of Bishop Chappel. William Mompesson died while on a visit to his nephew and was buried at Waddington, Lincolnshire, in April, 1737.

The Mompessons were surrogates and granted marriage licences, with the result that whilst they were vicars people from outside the parish came and were married here, turning Mansfield into a miniature Gretna Green.

'Vinegar Stones'   Referring to Mompesson's Well, J. B. Firth (Highways & Byways of Derbyshire) says:- 'A similar spot used for a similar purpose bears the interesting name of Qualmstones at Sarden, in Oxfordshire, qualm being an old word for pestilence.'

In the Lincolnshire edition of the same series we read:- 'At Tothby under a weeping ash tree on the lawn in front of the old Manor House farm, is an interesting relic of bygone days. It is a stone about a yard square and half a yard thick, once shaped at the corners and with a socket in it. Evidently it is the base of an old church-yard, wayside, or market-cross of prereformation times, and it has been put to use later as a plague-stone, having been for that purpose placed on its edge and half-buried probably, and a hole seven inches by five, and two and a half inches deep, cut in the upper side. This was to hold vinegar into which the townspeople put the money they gave for the farm produce brought from the country in times of plague.'

Names of Victims.   Reference has been made to the 'plague register' and the following is the list of obituaries. It will be noted that no dates of burial are recorded for the six people who died during March, 1666, and the ten last recorded in October. No reason appears to have been specified for the omission.

September, 1665,

George Viccars	..	..	.. Sept. 7	Thomas Thorpe	.. ..	Sept. 26
Edward Cooper	..	..	.. ,, 22	Sarah Sydall	.. .. ..	,, 30
Peter Halksworth	..	..	.. ,, 23	Mary Thorpe	.. .. ..	,, 30

October, 1665,

Matthew Bands	..	..	.. Oct. 1	Martha Bands	.. ..	Oct. 17
Elizabeth Thorpe	..	..	,, 1	Jonathan Ragge	.. ..	,, 18
Margaret Bands	..	..	,, 3	Humphrey Torre	.. ..	,, 19
Mary Thorpe	..	..	,, 3	Thomas Thorpe	.. ..	,, 19
Sythe Torre	..	..	,, 6	Mary Bands	.. ..	,, 20
William Thorpe	..	..	,, 7	Elizabthe Sydall	.. ..	,, 22
Richard Sydall	..	..	,, 11	Alice Ragge	.. ..	,, 23
William Torre	..	..	,, 13	Alice Sydall	.. ..	,, 24
Alice Torre (his wife)	..	..	,, 13	George Ragge	.. ..	,, 26
John Sydall	..	..	,, 14	Jonathan Cooper	.. ..	,, 28
Ellen Sydall	..	..	,, 15	Humphrey Torre	.. ..	,, 30
Humphrey Halksworth	..	..	,, 17			

November, 1665,

Hugh Stubbs	..	..	.. Nov. 1	Ann Stubbs (his wife) ..	..	Nov. 19
Alice Teylor	..	..	.. ,, 3	Elizabeth Warrington ..	..	,, 29
Hannah Rowland	..	..	,, 5	Randoll Daniel ..	.. ..	,, 30
John Stubbs	..	..	.. ,, 15			

December, 1665,

Mary Rowland	..	..	..	Dec.	1	William Rowe .. .. Dec. 19
Richard Coyle	..	..	..	,,	2	Thomas Willson .. .. ,, 22
John Rowbotton	..	..	..	,,	9	William Rowbottom .. .. ,, 24
– Rowe (an infant)	..	..	..	,,	14	Anthony Blackwell .. .. ,, 24
Mary Rowe	..	..	..	,,	15	

January, 1666,

Robert Rowbottom	..	..	Jan.	1	John Thornley .. .. .. Jan. 28
Samuel Rowbottom	..	..	,,	1	Isaac Willson .. .. .. ,, 28
Abell Rowland	..	..	,,	15	

February, 1666,

Peter Mortin, Bretton	..	..	Feb.	4	Alice Willson .. .. .. Feb. 18
Thomas Rowland	..	..	,,	13	Adam Halksworth .. .. ,, 18
John Willson	..	..	,,	15	Anthony Blackwell .. .. ,, 21
Deborah Willson	..	..	,,	17	Elizabeth Abell .. .. .. ,, 27

March, 1666

Jon. Thos. Willson	..	..	Mar.	—	Mary Buxton, Foolow .. Mar. —
John Talbot	..	..	,,	—	Ann Blackwell .. .. .. ,, —
John Wood	..	..	,,	—	Alice Halksworth .. .. ,, —

April, 1666,

Thomas Allen	..	..	April	6	Samuel Hadfield .. .. April 18
Joan Blackwell	..	..	,,	6	Margaret Gregory .. .. ,, 21
Alice Thorpe	..	..	,,	15	– Allen (an infant) .. .. ,, 28
Edward Bainsley	..	..	,,	16	Emmot Sydall .. .. .. ,, 30
Margaret Blackwell	..	..	,,	16	

May, 1666,

Robert Thorpe	..	..	May	2	James Taylor .. .. .. May 11
William Thorpe	..	..	,,	2	Ellen Charlesworth .. .. ,, 24

June, 1666,

Isaac Thornley	..	..	June	2	Sarah Lowe .. .. .. June 17
Anna Thornley	..	..	,,	12	Mary Mellow .. .. .. ,, 18
Jonathan Thornley	..	..	,,	12	Anna Townsend .. .. ,, 19
Anthony Skidmore	..	..	,,	12	Abel Archdale .. .. ,, 20
Elizabeth Thornley	..	..	,,	15	Edward Thornley .. .. ,, 22
James Mower	..	..	,,	15	Ann Skidmore .. .. ,, 25
Elizabeth Buxton	..	..	,,	15	Jane Townsend .. .. ,, 25
Mary Heald	..	..	,,	16	Emmot Heald .. .. ,, 26
Francis Thornley	..	..	,,	17	John Swanna .. .. ,, 29
Mary Skidmore	..	..	,,	17	

July, 1666,

Elizabeth Heald	July 2		Thomas Ashe	July 18
William Lowe	,, 2		William Thornley	,, 19
Eleanor Lowe (his wife)	,, 3		Francis Wood	,, 22
Deborah Ealott	,, 3		Thomas Thorpe	,, 22
George Darby	,, 4		Robert Thorpe	,, 22
Anna Coyle	,, 5		Robert Talbot	,, 24
Briget Talbot, Riley	,, 5		John Nealor	,, 25
Mary Talbot, Riley	,, 5		Thomas Healley	,, 25
John Dannyel	,, 5		Richard Talbot	,, 25
Elizabeth Swanna	,, 6		John Nealor	,, 26
Mary Thornley	,, 6		Joan Talbot	,, 26
John Townsend	,, 7		Ruth Talbot	,, 26
Ann Talbot, Riley	,, 7		Anna Chapman	,, 26
Francis Wragge	,, 8		Lydia Chapman	,, 26
Elizabeth Thorpe	,, 8		Margret Allen	,, 29
Elizabeth Lowe	,, 9		John Torre	,, 29
Edytha Thorpe	,, 9		Samuel Ealott	,, 29
Anne Lowe	,, 13		Rowland Mower	,, 29
Margaret Teylor	,, 14		Thomas Barkinge	,, 30
Alice Thornley	,, 16		Nicholas Whitby	,, 30
Jane Naylor	,, 16		Jonathan Talbot	,, 30
Edytha Barking	,, 17		Mary Whitby	,, 30
Elizabeth Thornley	,, 17		Rowland Mower	,, 30
Jane Talbot	,, 17		Sarah Ealott	,, 31
Robert Whyteley	,, 18		Joseph Allen	,, 31
Catherine Talbot	,, 18		Ann Mortin, Bretton	,, 31
Thomas Heald	,, 18		Robert Kempe, Shepherd's	
Robert Torre	,, 18		Flat	,, 31
George Short	,, 18			

August, 1666

George Ashe	Aug. 1		Richard Thorpe	Aug. 6
Mary Nealor	,, 1		Thomas Frith	,, 6
John Hadfield	,, 2		John Yealot	,, 7
Robert Bunton	,, 2		Oner Hancock	,, 7
Ann Naylor	,, 2		John Hancock	,, 7
Jonathan Naylor	,, 2		William Hancock	,, 7
Elizabeth Glover	,, 2		Abraham Swinnerton	,, 8
Alexander Hadfield	,, 3		Alice Hancock	,, 9
Jane Nealor	,, 3		Ann Hancock	,, 10
Godfrey Torre	,, 3		Francis Frith	,, 10
John Hancock, jun.	,, 3		Elizabeth Kempe	,, 11
Elizabeth Hancock	,, 3		William Halksworth	,, 12
Margaret Buxton	,, 3		Thomas Kempe	,, 12
Robert Barkinge	,, 3		Francis Bocking	,, 13
Margaret Percival	,, 4		Richard Bocking	,, 13
Annie Swinnerton	,, 4		Mary Bocking	,, 13
Rebecca Mortin, Shepherd's			John Tricket	,, 13
Flat	,, 4		Ann Trickett (his wife)	,, 13
Robert French	,, 6		Mary Whitbey	,, 13

Sarah Blackwall, Bretton	Aug.	13
Bridget Naylor	,,	13
Robert Hadfield	,,	14
Margaret Swinnerton	,,	14
Alice Coyle	,,	14
Thurston Whitbey	,,	15
Alice Bocking	,,	15
Briget Talbot	,,	15
Michael Kempe	,,	15
Ann Wilson	,,	15
Thomas Bilston	,,	16
Thomas Frith	,,	17
Joan French	,,	17
Mary Yealot	,,	17
Sarah Mortin, Shepherd's Flat	,,	18
Elizabeth Frith	,,	18
Ann Yealot	,,	18
Thomas Ragge	,,	18
Ann Halksworth	,,	19
Joan Ashmore	,,	19
Elizabeth Frith	Aug.	20
Margaret Mortin	,,	20
Ann Rowland	,,	20
Joan Buxton	,,	20
Frances Frith	,,	21
Ruth Mortin	,,	21
– Frith (an infant)	,,	22
Lydia Kempe	,,	22
Peter Hall, Bretton	,,	23
– Mortin (an infant)	,,	24
Katherine Mompesson	,,	25
Samuel Chapman	,,	25
Ann Frith	,,	25
Joan Howe	,,	27
Thomas Ashmore	,,	27
Thomas Wood	,,	28
William Howe	,,	30
Mary Abell	,,	30
Catherine Talbot	,,	30
Francis Wilson	,,	30

September, 1666,

Elizabeth Frith	Sept.	1
William Percival	,,	1
Robert Trickett	,,	2
Henry Frith	,,	3
John Wilson	,,	4
Mary Darby	,,	4
William Abell	,,	7
George Frith	,,	7
Godfrey Ashe	,,	8
William Halksworth	,,	9
Robert Wood	,,	9
Humphrey Merril	,,	9
Sarah Wilson	Sept.	10
Thomas Mozley	,,	16
Joan Wood	,,	16
Mary Percival	,,	18
Francis Mortin	,,	20
George Butterworth	,,	21
Ann Townsend, Bretton	,,	22
Ann Glover	,,	23
Ann Hall	,,	23
Francis Halksworth	,,	23
– Townsend (an infant)	,,	29
Susanna Mortin	,,	29

October, 1666,

James Parsley	Oct.	1
Grace Mortin	,,	2
Peter Ashe	,,	4
Abram Mortin	,,	5
Thomas Torre	,,	—
Benjamin Mortin	,,	—
Elizabeth Mortin	,,	—
Alice Teylor	Oct.	—
Ann Parsley	,,	—
Agnes Sheldon	,,	—
Mary Mortin	,,	—
Samuel Hall	,,	—
Peter Hall	,,	—
Joseph Mortin	,,	—

Historical Plaques. In the early paragraphs of the Guide chapters, reference was made to the doubtful information on plaques displayed at several sites in the village. The Parish Council has revised the text of some of these and the artistic work has been tastefully carried out by Mr. Philip Toft, the cost being shared by the Eyam Sports Association and the Peak Park Board. Incidentally, the village has now been declared a conservation area.

The Plague Cross at Ross-on-Wye. Visitors to Ross-on-Wye may be familiar with the story of C. John Kyrle, a 17th century benefactor of the church and town whose memory has been perpetuated in poetry by Alexander Pope as 'the Man of Ross.' But I would nominate a 17th century clergyman as being equally worthy of such a title. He was vicar of the town and was the Rev. John Price, who, when plague broke out in 1637, remained to comfort and counsel his sick parishioners when a colleague, who was rector at the time, followed the example of rich parishioners who fled the town to escape infection. He conducted the burial of victims by torchlight when they were interred during the night without coffins and in their own clothes. He courageously carried out the ministration of visiting the sick, administering the Sacrament and consoling the bereaved. At the peak of the epidemic, he urged the members of his flock to share with him in penitence and prayer as an act of repentance and reconciliation, and at five o'clock one morning a slow procession was seen winding its way down the High Street and past the Market Place singing the Litany. From that time of public intercession, the sufferings of the survivors were relieved and the epidemic ceased

On the plinth of an ancient cross in the churchyard, west of which was the communal grave in which most of the 315 victims were interred, is the inscription: *'Plague Ane Dom,* 1637, *Burials* 315. *Libera nus Domine.'* The area has never since been disturbed by subsequent burials.

Nan Scott's Chamber. It was in 1666 that the town of Newark in Nottinghamshire lost a third of its population by plague, and at the nearby village of Holme a fugitive from the disease took sanctuary in a room built above the church porch. This became known as Nan Scott's Chamber, recalling the old woman who sought sanctuary there, storing provisions sufficient for several weeks. From a window in the chamber, she was able to watch the frequent funerals of her friends and neighbours. When her supplies of food were exhausted, she had to visit the village to replenish her stock, and was horrified to find that, apart from one survivor, the population had been decimated by death and desertion. She hastily returned to the place of refuge and there spent the remainder of her days.

'They Lived .. they Loved .. they Died'. A sad story is related of Methven in A. R. Hope Moncrieff's 'Bonnie Scotland'.

'A beautiful spot is the Glen of Lynedoch, famed by a touching tradition which the graves of Bessie Bell and Mary Gray attest as no mere legend. These "bonnie lasses", as their song styles them, were bosom friends who beside the River Almond built themselves a bower of refuge from the Great Plague, raging in Perth as in London. According to the story, they were visited by a lover who brought them food, and with it the fatal infection. Prosaic critics point out that such bowers were used as isolation huts for suspected cases. At all events, the girls died in their hermitage, and were brought to be buried at Methven Church, but the Methven folk stoned back the bearers of contagion from the ford; then in death, as in life, the bodies found a home by the Almond. Their fate was so well though vaguely remembered that both Burns and Scott came to make enquiries about the grave, which had already been enclosed by the owner of the property, and is now marked by a railing, beneath a clump of yews, and by the inscription "They lived . . they loved . . they died".'

Cairn of the Dead. The Scottish village of Fortingall, renowned for its ancient yew tree and the claim that it is the birth-place of Pontius Pilate, has a tradition of the 14th century epidemic of the Black Death. In a field there is a memorial to a brave woman who, with the help of a white horse, dragged most of the victims from their homes to bury them at this site. Such was the extent of the mortality that the churchyard could no longer digest the swollen diet of death, and few survivors were left to deal with the problem, being either too weak or lacking in courage to cope with the accumulation of unburied corpses. But the old lady, instead of recoiling from the gruesome task, harnessed a white horse to a sledge on which she conveyed load after load of bodies to a mass grave near the village, completing the work by raising a cairn of earth and stones known as Carn-na-Marbh, or Cairn of the Dead, where a standing stone still indentifies the site.

Bridget Talbot's Bible: The assumption made previously that the Bridget Talbot, who bequeathed a Bible to four years' ols George Mompesson, was possibly sister-in-law to Richard Talbot of Riley Farm, may not be correct, but that she was his aunt. The bequest was made by 'Brigitt, ye relict of Mr. Robert Talbot' whose obituary is dated 16th August, 1666. Her husband had been Rector of Eyam from 1617 until his death and burial recorded '1630, August 20th, Buried Mr. Robert Talbot, Rector of Eyam.' This is the initial entry in Eyam's surviving parish register.

Many such records were lost or destroyed because of the casual way in which they had been kept since 1538 when they were instituted. This statutory order was treated with indifference by many parishes, and had to be further renewed in 1547 and again in 1599. It was later stipulated that the records should be entered in a parchment book by a more efficient system of documentation than the haphazard method which must have applied in Eyam until a century later.

Hearth Tax for Eyam 1670. This tax was levied between 1662-89 and was an annual payment of 2/- per hearth. Householders paying a yearly rent of less than 20 shillings, or who possessed less than £10 in real or personal estate, were exempt. It does not help in estimating the surviving population after the Plague, but supplies a list of residents of the 76 properties in the parish.

Hearth Tax for Eyam
Michaelmas 1670

Name	No. of hearths	Name	No. of hearths
Robert Eyre	9	Will Baxter	—
Mary Rowland	1	Antho: Raworth	1
Dorothy Cowlishaw	1	John Coe	1
George Johnson	1	Will Ainesworth	1
John Hawksworth	1	Jo: Wilson	1
Tho: Chapman sen.	1	Tho: Wragg	1
John Drable	1	Robert Thorpe	1
Ann Merrill	1	Katherine Wilson	1
George Plats	1	Bridget Ash	1
John Hall	1	Mr. Mompesson	4
James Moore	3	Mr. Stanley	2
Edw. Taylor	1	Stephen Wild	2
John Danyell	1	John Abell	1
Nicholas Danyell	1	Francis Whitacre	1
Tho: Danyell	2	Tho: Taylor	1
John Hardy	1	Rich: Bockinge	1
John Ragg	2	Tho: Heath	1
Rowland Wilson	1	Nicolas Thornley	1
Robert Fiddler	1	Francis Bockinge	1
Rich: Saxelby	1	Will Fryth	2
Margaret Dillington	1	Godfrey Torr	1
Martyn Furnisse	3	Stephen French	1
Annye Furnisse	1	Christopher Abell	1
Elizabeth Wood	1	Francis Torr	1
Francis Thornby	1	John Coates	1
Peter Bradshaw Esq.	7	Tho. Torr	1
Richard Furnisse	2	Phillip Sheldon	4
Francis Garret	1	George Talbot	1
Widd Skydmore	1	Whyteleyes House	1
Mary Wilson Widd	1	Robert Slyn	1
Willm Crane	1	Tho: Fryth	1
Roger Gregory	1	Jo: Taylor	1
Will Wilson	4	Will Knowles	1
Robt: Fox	1	Row: Merrill	1
Francis Blackwall	1	Tho: Wild	1
Jo: Swindle	1	Robt: Hill	1
Alice Rowland	2	Matthew Morton	1
Tho Wright Gent	4		
Henry Fanshaw	—		

Total 76 Houses

Religious Census (1676) lists Conformists (526), Papists (3) and Nonconformists (3).

Early Commemoration Service, Cucklett Dell, Eyam, August 27th, 1911

The Spar Queen

Eyam Cinerary Urn

THE AUTHOR EXAMINES A SPECIMEN OF LOCAL CORAL

MOMPESSON'S
CHAIR

RECTORY
STAIRCASE

EYAM

CHURCH

17th CENTURY
RECTORY

MRS.
MOMPESSON'S
TOMB

C. DANIEL

96

EYAM DISCOVERY TRAIL

*A Trail illustrating the Epic of Eyam Plague
and other aspects of the Village's History.
With line drawings of Bygone Eyam designed for
colouring with paints, pastels or crayons.*

By Clarence Daniel

'In Aiune (Eyam) Caschin held 2 caracutes of land (assessed) to the geld, (There is) land for 2 ploughs. (Wood) land for pannage 1 league in breadth. In King Edward's time it was worth 20 shillings and (is worth the same) now'. Domesday Book 1088.

Other spellings of the word Eyam, which is derived from a combination of the Anglo-Saxon words 'ey' meaning water and 'ham' a home, occur in documents as follows:- A.D. 1216-72 Aium (Index Locurum), Eium (Derbyshire Charters), 1248 Eyum (Derbyshire Charters), 1275 Eyam (Rotuli Hundredorum), 1332 Eyom (Calendar of Inquisitions), 1393 Eyoum (Derbyshire Charters), 1408 (Calendar of Inquisitions), 1428 Eyme and 1431 (Feudal Aids), 1746 Ayome (Derbyshire Charters), 1594 Eame (Index Locorum). Other renderings are Eham, Eam, Eme, Whyam, Hame and Hme.

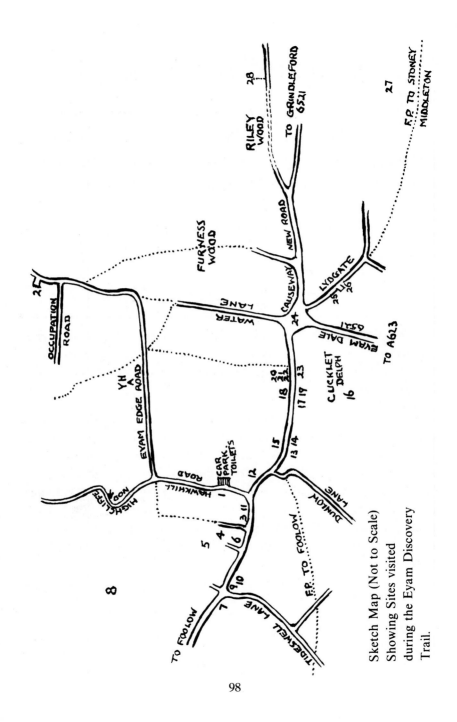

Sketch Map (Not to Scale)
Showing Sites visited
during the Eyam Discovery
Trail.

Bradshaw Hall (early 20th century)

STARTING FROM THE CAR PARK

Upon leaving the car-park, we note the crumbling ruins of BRADSHAW HALL (1) behind the Methodist Church. Built as a wing of Stafford Hall by Francis Bradshaw — who was descended from one of the three brothers of the regicide John Bradshaw — it is said to have been deserted by the family at the outbreak of the Plague. It was listed in 1670 (Hearth Tax returns) as having seven hearths and owned by Peter Bradshaw. Tradition says that tapestries rotted away without being hung. It later served as a cotton factory (when it was damaged by fire), and the buildings were later still applied to agricultural uses.

Turning right, we proceed up the hill for about 250 yards to a point where the road turns abruptly to the right. (Note: MOMPESSON'S WELL (2) is situated about ¾ of a mile up this road and may be reached by car, if necessary. The well is situated in a sloping cul-de-sac shortly after the Bretton road branches left. The latter road derives its present name 'Occupation Road' from the fact that it provided occupation to unemployed workers during a period of recession in local industry. It was fringed by enclosure portions awarded during the Eyam Enclosure Act of 1803.)

For the purposes of this Trail, however, we turn left just past the semi-detached houses, following the walled footpath of May Walk, noting at the bottom of the field to our left, the semi-circular elevation of HAWK HILL (3) where the Staffords and Bradshaws engaged in the sport of falconry. Passing through the stile, we see a row of cottages built of local sandstone and roofed with slabs of laminated shale from the now redundant 'slate quarries'. As we tour the village, we shall see that many houses and other buildings are roofed with this indigenous 'slate', and it will be noted that they vary in size from the eaves up to the ridges, each grade being given distinctive names such as 'large short honour' at the eaves with 'embore', 'wibbet', 'bachelor', 'middle-back', 'three dots', 'job' and 'mount' until 'farewell' is reached at the summit of the ridge. Known as AUDREY COTTAGES (4), a parallel row was demolished some years ago and were factories when cotton spinning was a major industry in the locality. When this industry became extinct because of the introduction of the power loom, and Eyam had no reliable supply of water, the factories were adapted to the manufacture of childrens' shoes. Children apprenticed to cotton manufacturers often lived on the premises and a record (1807) tells of an inspection by Dr. J. Denman, a Stoney Middleton magistrate, who reported on the factories of Messrs. Gregg & Co. and Messrs. Daintry & Co., the latter employing about 90 adults.

Continuing down the path, passing on our right the blank wall of two houses in which we note blocked up doors and arched windows which remind us that these premises were originally used for industrial purposes, we soon join the main road at the Royal Oak and there turn right. A short distance up the road, and standing modestly back from the road, is the BIRTHPLACE of RICHARD FURNESS (6), Eyam's poet and carol-maker. Built in 1615 this house was the scene of both Quaker and Methodist persecution. It was later the place of departure for the twice weekly coach service to Sheffield as described by R. Murray Gilchrist, the Victorian novelist, in his 'Milton' stories.

Turning up the lane past Gothic House, we pass between farm buildings to a stile into the field where we see the TOMB of HUMPHREY MERRIL (5) who died of plague on the 9th Sept., 1666. Probate was granted to his widow, Ann, when his domestic goods and farm stock were valued at £40 3s. 6d. His sheep were estimated at £9., his horses £2 10s., and five cows, two bullocks and two little stirks £14 16s. 8d. Returning to the main road we continue up to the Townhead factory of RALPH WAIN (7) who discovered the revolutionary process of weaving silk to reproduce the design on both sides of the fabric. Unable to read or write, he forfeited the credit for his invention which was patented by a Macclesfield firm to whom he sold the rights. The factory since has been adapted to the making of shoes, climbing pitons, printing, and clock cases.

Looking across to the escarpment of Eyam Edge we see the distant spoil heaps of the long redundant HIGHCLIFFE MINE (8) partially hidden among the trees on the hillside. This lead-mine was once famous for the incidence of the mineral phenomenon known variously as slickensides, crackingwhole and looking-glass. This was caused during the geological process of faulting when opposing rock surfaces were under such immense pressure that they were smeared with a thin veneer of galena, giving a highly polished and fluted effect. Explosions, often caused by the stroke of a miner's pick or hammer, were due to the sudden release of stresses created by movements of the strata. Tools were improvised from wood to prevent possible 'ignition' of the slicken-sides and sacks of moss were used to cushion the explosions.

Returning down the village street, we notice a much renovated cottage at the junction of Tideswell Lane which incorporates the village PINFOLD (9) in its garden complex. Here stray cattle were impounded by the 'pinner' or 'poundsman' and owners had to pay a fee for the recovery of the animals. This

Royal Oak (before restoration)

cottage is the reputed home of MARSHALL HOWE (10), a lead-miner who acted as self-appointed plague sexton and who carried out his duties with little reverence or respect for the victims he buried. He performed this task for his wife, Joan, on the 27th August and three days later for his only son, William.

As we retrace our steps down from the Town Head, passing the Royal Oak we note one of the four village smithies which supplied shoes for horses, iron tyres for cart-wheels, plough shares, shovels, and other wrought-iron work for farmers, lead-miners and quarrymen. At this point, the Jumber Brook flows underground beneath Fiddler's Bridge, probably named after the family to which Robert Fidler belonged. He was one of the assayers who helped to estimate the goods of plague victims, and whose signature (or mark) appears in endorsement of several inventories compiled after the Plague. The cottages standing on rising ground to our left occupy a site where the orchards of the Stafford-Bradshaw families flourished on the slopes of their hawk-hill, and are recalled by the name ORCHARD BANK (11). It was from one of these cottages that a young woman made an abortive attempt to escape the plague by fleeing to Tideswell, a distance of five miles. It was market day when the venture was planned, and she succeeded in evading the vigilance of parish constables appointed to keep watch and ward at entries to the township. The normal population was swollen by the weekly influx of farmers trading their cattle; dairy maids selling butter, eggs, cheese and poultry; together with hucksters, pedlars and market traders displaying their wares to tempt the pockets and purses of buyers from surrounding villages. The fugitive mingled furtively with the crowd, but was recognised by an acquaintance, whereupon the cry 'The plague! the plague! a woman from Eyam' was on every lip and the poor woman was chased by a furious mob flinging stones, sticks, turf and other missiles to encourage her departure.

Descending the Thorne, we notice that the antique shop on our left is built upon an outcrop of limestone. It figures upon one of the earliest post-card views of Eyam, and then had a thatched roof. The ruins of Bradshaw Hall can be glimpsed up the cart-track just beyond. Further down, before the road bends sharply right, a bay windowed house was the shop belonging to Ralph Wain who, like other silk weavers, owned a farm and shop where employees were expected to obtain their groceries and other supplies. The three principal weaving factories belonged to Ralph Wain, James Slinn and Wm. Froggatt & Sons in 1857, and, although none appears to have issued trade tokens to be used by their personnel, they each offered this benefit. Descendants of Ralph had a mineral factory where cherryade, lemonade and other soft drinks were produced to refresh visitors to Eyam. When the factory

Orchard Bank (last century)

104

was demolished, two brothers used the bricks for interior walls of the semi-detached houses they built from sandstone quarried and dressed from the parish quarry at Shay Corner.

Across the road, just past the butcher's shop, is an attractive house said to have been occupied at the time of the Plague by MARGARET BLACKWELL (13) who is reputed to have recovered from the disease after drinking hot bacon fat when in a state of delirium.

Proceeding past the Post Office, White Shop and Rose & Crown, we pass Cussey (causeway) Lane which is used as the processional route to the Delph on Plague Sunday. As a matter of historical interest, we may note that the estate built by the West Derbyshire District Council derives its name from the fact that it was built on the New Close. The explanation of this name is that it was the earliest enclosure award in Eyam, dating to the early 17th century when it was the New Enclosure. The adjective in many such instances had relevance for the contemporary generations, but with the passage of time becomes a freak of nomenclature which future generations may fail to understand.

Reaching the Hall, we are now in the former market-place (note the cobbles remaining near the semi-circular steps approaching the Hall gates) with the MARKET-HOUSE (13) still standing near the stocks. It is the property of the Parish Council, which authority administers the area under the terms of a Trust established by the bequest of a former resident. The STOCKS (14) were provided in the first place by the Barmote Court for the punishment of lead-miners guilty of infringing its unique laws. Built by Thomas Wright, EYAM HALL (15) was completed in 1678 and its erection may have been halted by the Plague. Although Tudor in style of architecture, it appears to have been built largely in Stuart times.

To visit CUCKLET CHURCH (16), the limestone grotto where the Rev. William Mompesson held services after deciding to close the Parish Church for public worship, it is necessary to obtain a key from the Hall (application at the back door) for which a small charge is made. Admission to Cucklet Delph is by a gate in the railings near the stocks, and we pass near the forgotten site of the TOOTHILL (17) where pagan ceremonies were conducted in ancient times. The footpath leads down a steep descent, crosses the stream which emerges from the Salt Pan gorge and climbs the opposite bank and over the shoulder of this hill to reach the cavern where Mompesson gave counsel and encouragement to his shrinking flock. Upon retracing our steps, and returning the key, we continue down the street and opposite the hearth where sheep are roasted on Carnival Day, we see DELF VIEW (17), formerly the

Eyam Hall

106

home of Frederick Dawson, world famous pianist and rival of Paderewski, Polish musician and prime minister. The house has many literary associations, and it is here that Joseph Wright, the Derby artist, painted his portrait of Sarah Carver and her daughter which is included in the Wright collection of Derby Art Gallery. The plot of ground used on Carnival Day for the roasting of sheep and serving sandwiches, is shown on the engraving of Sir Francis Chantrey's drawing of the Plague Cottages, as a strip of water known as the Eaver End (since corrupted to River End). The area has since been drained, either in the interests of public safety or under the terms of an enclosure award. The two stone troughs were supplied for domestic water and for the use of horses and cattle to compensate for the loss of these facilities, and for which provision was made in the text of the Enclosure Awards.

A few paces along is the PLAGUE COTTAGE (18) central in a picturesque group of 17th century cottages. Here George Viccars, a journeyman tailor, lodged with a widow and her two sons, and here he received a consignment of cloth which proved to be infected with the bacteria of bubonic plague conveyed from far-off London. Tradition tells how he became the first victim (Sept. 7th, 1665) after having unpacked the cloth — damp after its long journey — and which he hung before the cottage fire to dry out. Two sons of the widow also died, but Mary Cooper survived and was later married to a lead-miner named Coe. Peter Halksworth, the third victim died in the cottage next door, and his widow Alice married Matthew Morton, of Shepherd's Flatt, who had been bereaved of his wife and family. Across the road is the cottage (formerly thatched) where EMMOT SYDDAL (19) figured in a tragic love drama with Rowland Torre. She was bereaved of her father, brother and four sisters during the early days of the Plague, and she herself fell victim on the last day of April, 1666. Her mother alone survived.

THE CHURCH (20) dedicated to St. Lawrence with a Chapel of St. Helen, has been much altered during its long history and contains both a Saxon and Norman front (the latter shorn or its original ornamentation by an over-zealous mason carrying out an instruction to clean off a coat of green paint). Although there is no reference to a church in the Domesday entry, there is evidence of Saxon work in the bases of the Norman pillars between the nave and north aisle. A series of wall paintings in the nave were uncovered during the late 19th century restoration, but were so defaced as to be judged unsuitable for preservation. But theses have since been 're-discovered' and subjected to a rescue operation by the use of modern techniques and treatment. Owing to the early closure of the church during the Plague, there

Plague Cottages (18th Century)

108

are few relics of that time, and the paper funeral garlands mentioned by Anna Seward have long since been destroyed. There is an illuminated list of the names of plague victims and also a list of clergy — including several titled rectors — who have held the Living. A Jacobean cupboard mounted on the wall of the north aisle has the dubious claim to be the chest in which the infected cloth travelled from London to Eyam in 1665. The actual chair of Mompesson is preserved in the chancel and approaches have been made to acquire a matching settle carved with his name and that of his wife, but have not been successful.

Built into the north wall is part of a stone coffin lid which was found in the Stafford vault when the Church was restored last century. It has been called St. Helen's Cross, and may have been used as a Cresset Lamp which stood on the altar of the chapel as a condition of tenure whereby the Staffords held land in the district. A Tudor bronze lamp hanging in the rector's vestry was presented earlier this century to the church with the apocryphal claim that it is the Lamp of St. Helen, but without evidence as to when or why it was removed from Eyam after the service of maintaining the lamp was abolished following the accession of King James. But even though the genuineness of this lamp cannot be verified, the actual condition dates to the 13th century and is attested by two Latin documents in the British Museum. One of the Staffords made a bequest of wax for its maintenance.

In his account of Derbyshire Churches, Dr. J. C. Cox says of Eyam, 'There was formerly a piscina at the east end of the north aisle, and an oblique opening at that angle, forming a "squint" for obtaining a view of the high altar in the chancel, but these have disappeared during the enlargement of this aisle.' (1868-9). The comment of Dr. Cox is incorrect in that the piscina still remains, but is supported by a plan made by the late Mr. William Dane showing the squint at that angle, and also the pulpit occupying the position where the lectern now stands. Canon J. M. J. Fletcher states, however, that 'the Squint, or opening in the wall through which the altar could be seen, at the east end of the south aisle, was for a long time filled up, but was re-opened on May 15th., 1908. The glass shutter on the chancel side was then added to keep out the draught.' A village mason assured the writer that he had cut through the masonry to provide the squint for the benefit of a family whose pew was situated in the south aisle, and that they had defrayed the cost.

The rector's vestry was original designed for the domestic accommodation of the Rev. Joseph Hunt (inducted March 1683) and his wife, Anne, 18 years' old daughter of Matthew Fearn, landlord of the Miners'

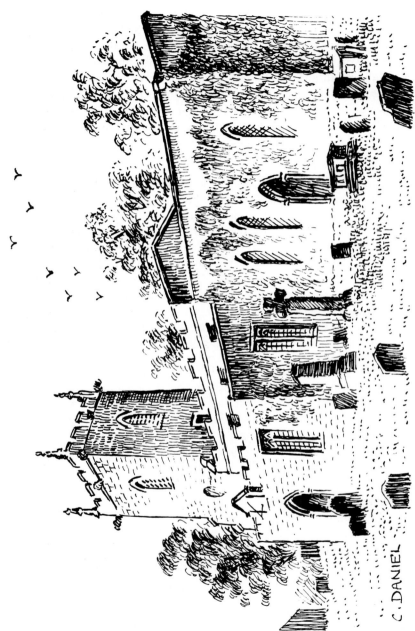

Eyam Church (before restoration)

Arms. The young couple had been involved in a mock marriage at the inn, and this had to be legally confirmed by order of the bishop of the diocese. Already engaged to a lady of some social status, the Rector was sued for breach of promise and finally had to vacate the rectory and seek asylum in the church to avoid arrest by bailiffs seeking to recover costs of the legal action. The rector's two daughters, Mary and Sarah, were born in the church and both he and his wife died and were buried in church to prevent their bodies being seized as payment of the long standing debt. The earliest existing parish register is a transcription he made from the original loose documents.

The windows of the building are worthy of inspection; one in the south aisle having the artist's signature represented by a spider's web, while one in the north aisle contains very old glass, and two in the chancel portray the actual features of the persons memorialised.

Passing into the churchyard, we note the headstone of Abell Rowland, an early victim of the plague. Over the chancel door is a fine 18th century sundial which formerly adorned the entrance to the church, and nearby is a white stone perpetuating the memory of the Rev. Thomas Stanley, Rector of Eyam until 1662, who worked along with Mompesson to restrain the spread of plague. He was a native of Duckmanton, near Chesterfield, and was one of the 2,000 clergy who left their pulpits and parishes in 1662. He made a number of wills for members of the stricken population. His actual grave is not known. Opposite is the SAXON or CELTIC CROSS (21); a fine example of primitive Christian art with its carved vine scrollery, interlaced knotwork and Christian symbolism.

The top part of the shaft, which may have had a carved panel to match the two beneath, is missing and was probably mutilated during the Commonwealth when vandalism of the sacred emblem was encouraged by Act of Parliament resulting in widespread desecration of ancient preaching and boundary crosses. It appears to have been restored by Canon Thomas Seward at the instigation of John Howard, the prison reformer. Its original site is unknown, but the village green known as 'The Cross', the eminence of Cross Low between Eyam and Foolow, and a site near the ancient Sir William Road, have variously been suggested. Near the cross is the TOMB of CATHERINE MOMPESSON (22), wife of the Rev. William Mompesson and a victim of the plague. A sufferer from consumption, she knowingly risked her life to give support to her husband when he elected to remain in the village to counsel and console his parishioners. Note how an error in the Latin inscription has been neatly corrected by a square of stone counter-sunk into the surface.

Main Road (last century)

Opposite the Church is the former MECHANICS' INSTITUTE (23) with its imposing portico supported by two massive gritstone pillars, reminding us of the educational facilities provided for mechanics and apprentices last century. It was opened on Jan. 11th., 1859, the inaugural address being given by Lord G. H. Cavendish M.P., supported by W. P. Thornhill M.P., Dr. Thomas Fentem (surgeon), T. Gregory Esq., (solicitor) and the Rector, The Hon. Robert Eden, who composed the original committee. It is now the Village Club. We proceed down the main road, passing the Rectory on our left. This building was re-modelled in 1960 when the imposing Georgian wing built during the days of lead-mining prosperity by Canon Seward was demolished. The earlier buildings with their historical associations, including the study, staircase and family rooms occupied during the dramatic days of the Plague, were retained and incorporated in the re-designed plan. The village school just below was opened in 1877, and some of the masonry from the demolished tower windmill was used in its construction. Token fruit trees were planted in the playground as a legal protection against possible tipping of hillock stuff from the adjacent Glebe, or Townend, Mine. It is possible that this mine was involved in the following unusual transaction: 'May 8th, 1723. Then George Cooper of Hunday bought one 6th part of a Groove called parson pippin in Eyam Lordship and all possessions of Isaac Wilde for 24 pecks of Mele and half a load of Wheat and 2 Strikes of Malt — Entered by me Edw. Morton, Barmaster.' Lead has been mined in the village since Saxon times, and the industry continues along with the extraction and processing of barytes and fluorspar which supplies material to chemical and other industries. The village has its ancient Barmote Court for the liberty of Stoney Middleton and Eyam.

Near the smaller traffic island in the Square, a small iron plate with finger-hole covers the BULL RING (24) where bulls and sometimes bears were formerly baited by dogs as a barbarous form of sport. In Chesterfield a bye-law could be invoked whereby butchers bringing bulls for slaughter were fined 3s. 4d. if they refused to have the animals baited. It was contended that this practice made the beef more tender.

Crossing the Square to the Lydgate, we walk up this lane and pass the former home of WILLIAM WOOD (25), the 19th century historian, who collected much information concerning the antiquities of Eyam and other aspects of its history. The name Lydgate is derived from 'covering gate' where the custom of keeping watch and ward during the hours of darkness was observed by a rota of able-bodied residents. They were charged with the security of the parish and, armed with halberd and lantern, they challenged any stranger seeking entry into the village during the hours from dusk to daylight. When a man had fulfilled his turn, he would leave the watch-bill and lantern at the door of his successor. Round the corner are the LYDGATE GRAVES (26) contained in an enclosure of the former Parson's Field. George Darby was a lead-miner who made his will on July 3rd., 1666, the day he actually died. His wife, Mary, and married daughter, Elizabeth, husband of Robert Slinne, and grandchild, Anne, survived the plague, but his single daughter, Mary, fell victim of the plague on September 4th, 1666. In a codicil to his will, he desires that his 'Grove' (lead-mine) should be equally divided between his wife and her namesake, together with turn-trees and other mining tools, but the daughter died on 4th September, after gathering flowers to lay on his grave. About fifty yards up the lane on the right side is Eyam Private Museum which is open by appointment (Hope Valley 31010), but not on Sundays.

Those wishing to visit the Plague BOUNDARY STONE (27) about half a mile towards Stoney Middleton, will continue to the top of the lane where a stile next to the gate facing us, gives access to a footpath through two fields, after which it becomes enclosed between two walls. Having skirted the spoil heaps of Cliff Stile Mine, we enter a large area which was formerly common land where isolation huts are recorded to have been built for the accommodation of plague victims. Following the footpath which continues directly across the field, we see a sandstone boulder on our left near a ring of trees. It is pierced with a pattern of holes in which money was placed in payment for medicines and other supplies needed by the quarantined villagers, vinegar being poured into the holes in the mistaken belief that this would sterilise the coins. Like many such plague landmarks in various townships and parishes visited by plague, it is sometimes called the Vinegar Stone or Penny Stone.

From this landmark, when the weather is favourable, we can see the village of Curbar lying beneath the escarpment of Curbar Edge. This former hamlet of Baslow was visited by plague in 1632, and the stones marking the graves of seven victims remain. These bear the initials of the victims together with the year of visitation, and a curious feature is that in each instance the numeral '3' is reversed.

As we return to the village, we may note the enclosure of Riley Graves in the narrow field on the hillside to our right, and discern the terraced foundations of the farmhouse and buildings of the Hancock family. Further left, the white walls of the gable and facade of the present Riley Farm arrest our attention and identifies the site of Richard Talbot's farm and smithy. A prosperous farmer and blacksmith, Talbot's will was composed by the Rev. Wm. Mompesson and is interesting for the fact that the Rector had to make an erasure in the first line due to the fact that he had mistakenly written his own name instead of that of the testator. The inventory of Talbot's husbandry and household goods is an interesting commentary on the time. With the exception of one son, Richard and his wife Catherine and five children died during July, 1666, and their family grave is marked by a tabular tombstone in the orchard which is in private ownership.

Students of geology will notice that some of the stiles consist of slabs of encrinital limestone, or Derbyshire Marble, and are polished smooth by the clothing and footwear of those who for centuries have used the path. Some people complain of the narrowness of the stiles, but they are intended to prevent sheep straying away from their pastures. There may be those interested to know that the footpath roughly follows the underground course of Moorwood Sough, an expensive project intended to drain the Edgeside Mines, but which was never completed although three companies invested considerable capital in the attempt.

Arriving back in the Square, we turn right and follow the Grindleford road to the edge of the village where a gated lane on our left leads through Riley Wood for nearly half a mile until we see RILEY GRAVES (28) in a field on our left. The enclosure is reached by a stile and is the property of the National Trust. Here Elizabeth Hancock buried her husband and six children during a week in August, 1666. The actual grave of the father is identified by the central tomb with its quaint epitaph, but the headstones of the family were scattered about the field until they were collected and enclosed along with that of the father. After performing her nightmare task, Mrs. Hancock escaped to Sheffield where she found sanctuary with a surviving son who was apprenticed to the cutlery trade. The deserted farm and buildings are said to have fallen into ruin and disrepair until they were eventually demolished.

Returning to the village, we may note the Wesleyan Reform Church on our left. This is a typical example of early Methodist architecture, and was built on the site of several cottages in 1798, shortly after the death of John Wesley. With its arched windows, stout walls and gallery, it agrees with the design generally approved by Wesley on the assumption that the pulpit should occupy a central position above the communion table because the ministry of the prophet was superior to that of the priest. The row of houses opposite have been both a cotton-mill and a shoe factory.

EXTRACT FROM A SIX DAY'S RAMBLE
OVER DERBYSHIRE HILLS AND DALES
IN THE YEAR 1858

by Richard Keene

MONDAY

Eyam, standing on a rocky platform of considerable elevation, is approached by the steep winding road which runs up the rocky chasm of Eyam Dale, some half-mile in length ; and glad were we when the top was reached. It was seven o'clock before we arrived at Mrs. Fox's, where we had arranged to stay during our sojourn at Eyam ; and after despatching a hearty tea, which included some genuine Derbyshire oat cake, we set out for an evening stroll, under the guidance of Mr. Wood. Passing along the western portion of the village, we visited the tomb of Humphrey Merril, which stands in a field about half-a-mile to the north-west of the church. The sun had set, and a gentle breeze, laden with the scent of new-made hay, stirred the grass that waved round this lone tomb. While contemplating the fate of Humphrey Merril, and listening to the quiet, but clear and interesting account of the plague from our friend, a pensive feeling came over us, and we could not but admire the heroic spirit and the self sacrificing principle which had induced him, through all the horrors of the pestilence, calmly to await his own doom sooner than be the means of spreading the contagion to other parts of the country. All honour be to the memory of this brave man and his compatriots ; peace to their ashes and rest to their souls ! By the twilight gleam, on the end of his tomb we could discern the initials " H. M., 1666." He died on the ninth of September, one of the latest victims.

Retracing our steps till we came nearly to the Hall, we turned off to Cucklett Dell, or the Delf as it is commonly called, the

upper ground of which we explored by the dim evening light, as
far as its junction with Middleton Dale. Cucklett Church*
was shrouded in shadow, and, standing beneath its rocky arches,

CUCKLETT CHURCH.

we could scarcely see between the dark overhanging branches of
the surrounding trees to the bottom of the Dell :

" So hushed, so shrouded its deep bosom lies."

At the extremity of this secluded ravine, on the point of rock
guarding its eastern entrance, we had a most beautiful view of
Middleton Dale, though perhaps too dark to show it to the best
advantage. Wending our way back again by the same rough
route, through the long and dewy grass, we next went to the
churchyard, just to notice the positions of the cross, Catherine
Mompesson's tomb, etc., so that we might arrange for the
morrow. It was a glorious evening, and with pleasant remini-
scences of a former visit, I proposed a walk through the village
and on to the Sheffield Road, towards the Riley graves, and we

---

* " Cucklet, or Cuckletts, is the name of certain fields, or plots of land,
west of the rock where Mompesson preached ; the name is said to be a corrup-
tion of the words, Cook's Lot,—that is, land that once belonged to a family
named Cook."—*Wood.*

soon found ourselves on this elevated highway overlooking a vast stretch of country ; we

" Saw the hills
Grow larger in the darkness."

Down in the vale at our feet lay Middleton, half shrouded in the assembling mists, through which twinkled many a cottage light ; while above all in the calm sky we watched the red moon rising to assume her starry throne. It was a scene not easily forgotten, and, had we no thought for the morrow, should doubtless have wandered a good way further. It was half-past nine when we reached our cottage.

Supper in Mrs. Fox's old-fashioned room, and a chat over our tobacco with her, round the fire, was not the least pleasant sensation of the day. This cottage where we were staying stands at a short distance to the west of the church, and next to the house where the plague broke out in the memorable 1665 ; indeed it is under the same roof, and was built at the same time. The walls are of immense thickness and well built, the floors are of stone nicely sanded, and the roof is covered with the same material ; it would almost seem as if it was intended to stand as long as the rock on which it is built. Inside, the walls are washed with a bright blue colour (a favourite fashion in the Peak), and behind our venerable hostess hangs a row of glittering household utensils ; an antique clock ticks against the wall, surmounted by a curious old jug made in the shape of a bear, a great curiosity, and as ancient as the clock ; a bright fire-place and good fire ; the door open till late in the night, whereat the jessamine peeps in and nods its star-like flowers ; and the four travellers round the fire, kicking up their slippered feet, complete the picture. Old Mrs. Fox* is telling us stories of by-gone days, and puffing at intervals her long clay pipe, which she seems thoroughly to enjoy. The air grows chill, the door is closed, and we sit till midnight listening to our ancient friend's details of the plague, the gibbet

* Mrs. Fox died June 4, 1872, at the advanced age of 96.

on Wardlow Mires, and other interesting matters connected with the locality. Having spent the greater part of her life in the village, she has handed down many of the traditions of the plague, which Mr. Wood has embodied in his interesting History of Eyam. Amongst the stories we heard, she told us how, many years back, through burning the Christmas holly (which was a very unlucky thing to do !), a chimney took fire in the next house, where the plague had first appeared, and that it made the wall of her bedroom so hot that she could not bear her hand on it ; that a sort of wooden flue, or passage for steam from the copper opened into the chimney ; this getting on fire, was hastily chopped down, when a pair of old leathern stays fell therefrom. These stays were very heavy, and she supposes full of money sewed in them, and that they were hidden there in the time of the plague, instead of being burnt, as was most of the clothing. She never saw them again, and her neighbour said they were burnt for fear of infection ; but he soon after left the house and appeared in much better circumstances. Thus, instead of ill-luck, the burning of the holly proved a very fortunate event for him.

We heard the midnight hour toll from the neighbouring church before we retired to rest.

TUESDAY.

" AMONG the verdant mountains of the Peak,
  There lies a quiet hamlet, where the slope
  Of pleasant uplands wards the north-winds bleak ;
  Below, wild dells romantic pathways ope ;
  Around, above it, spreads a shadowy cope
  Of forest trees ; flower, foliage, and clear rill
  Wave from the cliffs, or down ravines elope ;
  It seems a place charmed from the power of ill
  By sainted words of old :—so lovely, lone, and still."

WE rose soon after six o'clock, and while breakfast was preparing I strolled out in my slippers to the churchyard—one of the prettiest I know.* Fine rows of limes surround it, and as I stood meditating beneath their scented boughs, the hum of myriads of bees rifling the sweet bunches of flowers fell on my ear,

"Like sound with which a dream is filled."

Truly this is an interesting and sacred spot, and to a thoughtful mind, full of the most thrilling associations : the runic cross with its interlaced knot-work and rude figures carrying one back in imagination to the days of good King Alfred ; the church itself,

EYAM CHURCH.

though little is left of its original work, has witnessed many changes that have been wrought in this land ; but its chief charm

---

* Wood, in his last edition of the History of Eyam (1868), says :—" The churchyard, as well as the village, are fast losing their Stoke Poges characteristics. Increase of population, and the introduction of trades, will soon obliterate every trace of the old English village."

lies in having been the scene of the worthy Mompesson's labours, and the burial-place of his dear wife, Catherine —

" Where tears have rained, nor yet shall cease to flow."

—and many other victims of the plague.

After a quiet stroll about the churchyard, looking at the famous dial over the porch, and taking a general survey, I joined my friends at the breakfast table, where we did ample justice to the eggs and bacon prepared for us. Thus primed for a good day's work, we commenced in the churchyard, taking several views, including a good one of the cross. Our next picture was a view of Eyam, looking west. Mr. Wood, who had again joined us, showed us at the east end of the village, at the rear of his house, in a small meadow, two flat gravestones to the memory of the Darbys, victims of the plague. Continuing our walk eastward, we visited the Riley graves, the approach to which is by a road branching off the Sheffield turnpike, about a quarter-of-a-mile from the village, through a plantation ; the golden gorse, the graceful harebell, and the stately foxglove decorating the sandy banks on either side. Emerging from the shade of the trees into the open fields, ascending all the while, we soon came to the Riley graves. They stand on the steep slope of the hill, in the middle of a field, and are surrounded by a rude wall, in shape resembling a heart, which serves to protect them from the cattle ; nodding ferns and foxgloves springing up from the rank grass decorate this rude cemetery, where sleep the plague-stricken forms of John Hancock and his children. The view hence is extensive and beautiful, embracing a vast stretch of country right away to Masson, where it meets the horizon.

Never shall I forget the stroll to the Riley graves, nor how we lay on the grass basking in the sunshine, while William Wood narrated in his straightforward, earnest, and simple manner, how the poor mother buried her husband and family, as one after the other they died of the plague—how she was seen of the people in Stoney Middleton, to drag them one by one, by the aid of a towel tied to their feet, to the shallow graves she scooped out on the moorside—and he pointed out a tree some fifty or sixty yards off, where the house of the Hancocks stood at the time.

But we must up and away, after taking a stereogram of the

THE RILEY GRAVES.

graves, to the house of the Talbots, now called Riley Farm House, some quarter-of-a-mile distant. The family of Talbot were all carried off before the Hancocks, and we saw the tabular tomb where they are interred in the orchard close to the house.

The inscriptions of these various tombs are all given by Wood in his exhaustive history, so that I shall not repeat them here.

We continued our walk on to the Moor, up a very rough road, high above Eyam, to see Mompesson's Well, as it is called, which consists of a stone, covering the source of a tiny mountain rivulet in a hollow on the left as we ascended, the upper surface of which is carved in the form of a cross. This was one of the points, on the imaginary line drawn around the village, which none were to pass, where provisions and other necessaries were brought for the villagers, and where the money used in the transactions was washed in the pure water of the spring, so that the contagion might not spread.* We returned by an upper road,

MOMPESSON'S WELL.

whence we had a fine view of Eyam, and passed through some fields with further memorials of the plague north of the church ;— the same fields where the young and beautiful Catherine Mompesson, the loving wife of the heroic rector, walked on the twenty-second of August, 1666, when she exclaimed to her husband what a sweet smell there was, and was immediately possessed by the plague, with which she struggled "for a few days, when her spirit took its flight to the regions of bliss." Our way continued through the churchyard, where we saw her tomb in

---

* Similar precautions were used at Derby in the time of the pestilence, a relic of which is now placed in the Arboretum, called the Headless Cross, which once stood upon Nun's Green.

a tolerably good state of preservation ; a yew tree had recently been planted at its foot.

There is a curious custom in this churchyard of placing stone pillars at the four corners of the tomb, as shown in the accompanying illustration.

The interior of Eyam Church contains but little worthy of notice.

After lunch, we went down Eyam Dale to take a picture of "The Haunted House." Truly it is an "unked" place ! and I suppose the scene of some outrage, which has caused its desertion and

EYAM DALE.

consequent decay. A gloomy sky and overhanging trees added to the melancholy of the spot, and we were not sorry to leave it for the more open part of the dale lower down, which is very picturesque. The woods of the Rock Gardens on one side, and the bold projections of limestone on the other, terminating with Blackwell Tor, a winding road and mumuring streamlet, the distance filled in with the green slopes of Middleton Pastures and the higher Moor, make up a fine picture. The "Golden Ball" public-house at the end of Eyam Dale, with Blackwell Tor in its rear, compose well, but the lime-kiln opposite was kicking up such a pother we could not take it. We turned to the right, and fighting our way through a luxuriant bed of nettles breast high, made our way into the Delf once more. It was getting almost too late to take photographs, but we secured one of Cucklett Church, from whose rocky arches Mompesson, after the church was closed in the time of the plague, was wont to address his daily-declining congregation as they stood or reclined apart from and afraid of each other.

> " Arch meeting arch, unwrought of human hands,
> Form dome and portals. On its roof the air
> Waves leafy boughs ; the Alpine flower expands ;
> It seems a spell-constructed bower."

BRADSHAW'S HOUSE.

It was too dark to get a view of the Salt-pan, as the narrow ravine at the upper end of this Dale is called, so we wended our way to Humphrey Merril's tomb, which we took in the dull evening light. Hollins House, where he lived, is only about a hundred yards distant.

A slight shower turned us homeward. On our way we noticed

the remains of President Bradshaw's House,* now used as a barn and cow-shed ; and finished the day's work at photographing with a view of the village looking east.

After tea I went again into the churchyard, and was copying inscriptions from gravestones till the wind and rain drove me indoors. We spent another cozy, chatty evening ; and, after talking over the next day's route, and regretting we could not bring in a visit to Wet-Within's Druidical circle on the Moor, went to bed rather earlier.

Amongst the inscriptions, I copied the following from a quaint tablet to the memory of Anne Sellars and her husband :—

Here Li'th
Ye Body of Anne Sellars   Bu
Ried by this Stone.   Who dy
ed on Jan.y. 15 Day 1731.
Likewise Here lise dear Jsaac
Sellars my Husband & my
Right.   Who was buried on
that Same Day Come seuen
years 1738.   In seuen years
time there Comes a Change
Obsarve and Here you'll See
On that same Day come
Seuen years my Husbands'
laid by Me.

Cunningham, a curate at Eyam near a century ago, has left behind him, on the tombstones in this churchyard, several specimens of his poetic ability. The following verses are said to have been written by him :—

To the Memory of
Edward, the son of
Thomas & Mary Froggatt
Who died December IV
A:D: MDCCLXXIX:
Aged XVIII years.

---

* See notice of this place by Mr. Furness, in *The Reliquary*, Vol. 2, p. 219.

> How eloquent the monumental stone,
> Where blooming, modest Virtues, prostrate lie !
> Where pure Religion from her hallow'd Throne,
> Tells man " it is an awful thing to Die."
>
> Is Happiness thy Aim ? Or Death thy Fear ?
> Learn how their Path with Glory may be trod,
> From the lamented Youth who slumbers here,
> Who gave the Flower of his Days to God.

The above is on a tombstone in the south-west part of the churchyard, near the path. At the east end of the church, " In memory of Sarah Cooper," is a stone with the following :—

> In sure and steadfast hope to rise,
> And claim her mansion in the skies,
> A Christian here her flesh laid down,
> The cross exchanging for a crown.
>
> Meet for the fellowship above
> She heard the call, Arise my love :
> I come, her dying looks replied,
> And lamb like as her Lord she died.

I also copied the inscription on the tomb of Catherine Mompesson :—

CATHERINA VXOR
GVLIELMI MOMPESSON
HVJUS ECCLESIÆ RECTS,
FILIA RADVLPHI CARR,
NVPER DE COCKEN IN
COMITATV DVNELMENSIS
ARMIGERI :
SEPVLTA VICESSIMO
QVINTO DIE MENSIS AVGTI.

AÑO. DNI. 1666.

127

Besides this, at the west end of the tomb is an hour-glass with wings and the words *Cavete nescitis horam* ; and at the east end a death's head with the motto, *Mors mihi lacrum.* The following inscription is from a lichen-stained stone placed by the east wall of the porch :—" Abell : the Sonne ʳ of . Thomas . & Alice Rowland . was bvried . Jan. the 15th 1665."

CATHERINE MOMPESSON'S TOMB.